BIRDBRAINS

BIRDBRAINS

A Lyrical Guide to
Washington State Birds

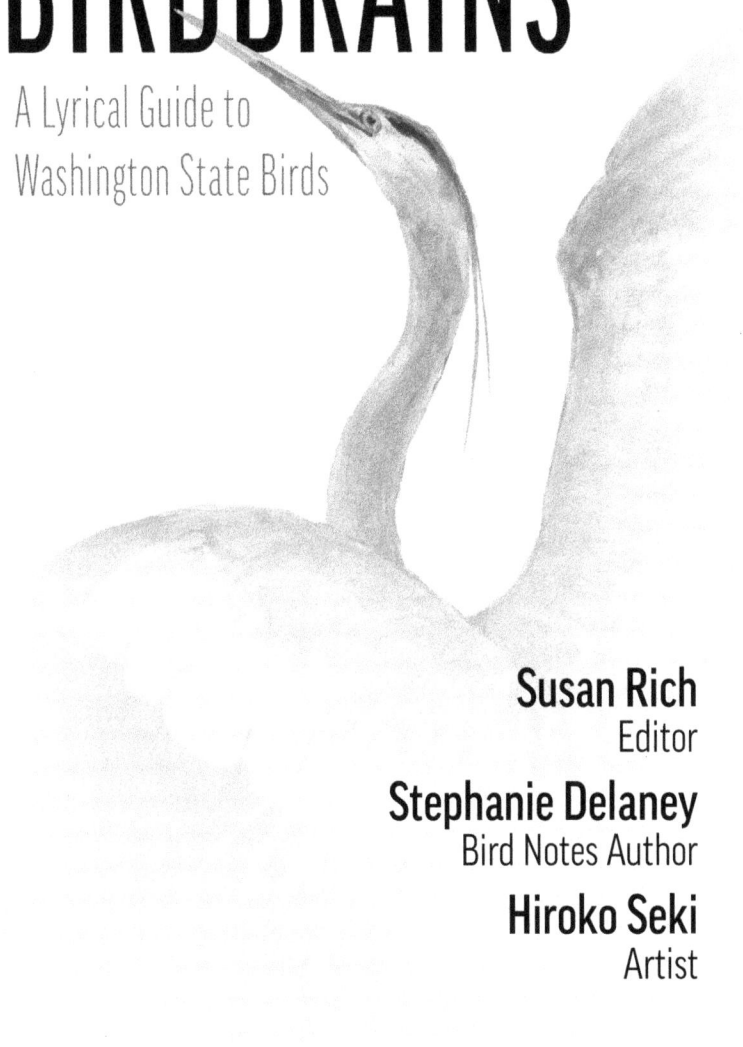

Susan Rich
Editor

Stephanie Delaney
Bird Notes Author

Hiroko Seki
Artist

RAVEN CHRONICLES
Corvus **PRESS** Corax

R A V E N
CHRONICLES PRESS

Printed in the United States of America
Copyright © 2025 Raven Chronicles Press/The Raven Chronicles

FIRST EDITION

Published in 2025
Printed in the United States of America.
ISBN: 978-1-7354780-9-8
Library of Congress Control Number: 2025939532

Cover Artwork: *Blue Heron with Plume,* Sumi-e Painting,
Hiroko Seki, 2025
Book & Cover Design: Tonya Namura
Back Cover Photo Credits:
Stephanie Delaney: Makers' Mercantile
Susan Rich: Rosanne Olson
Hiroko Seki: David Keller

Established in 1991, The Raven Chronicles is a Seattle-based
literary organization that publishes and promotes artistic work
and community events that embody the cultural diversity and
multitude of imaginations of writers and artists living in the
Pacific Northwest and other regions of the United States.

Raven Chronicles Press
15528 12th Avenue NE
Shoreline, Washington 98155-6226
editors@ravenchronicles.org
https://www.ravenchronicles.org

The thing that makes me happiest after poetry is birdwatching.

—Martha Silano

Dear Reader,

Here is a secret.

It was a brazen act to dream up this book. To tell you the truth, I am a novice with both binoculars and bird guides. And yet, with the earnestness of the recently converted, I persisted.

Call me a newbie, a beginner, a bird lover who sees Kingfishers and Northern Shovelers with wonderment. I suspect that many of you reading this page right now may feel the same. There is so much still to learn! Take away my Merlin App and I can't distinguish a Pine Siskin's song from that of a Bewick's Wren. In fact, I am convinced that I'm newer to the world of birding than most of the authors whose stellar work appears in this book.

No matter: rather than embarrassment, this turn of events makes me feel enlivened. According to Audubon journalist, Julia Zarankin, two recent scientific studies show that the more birds we humans hear, the happier we become. As birders, especially beginners, we intuitively know this: birdsong uplifts us, connecting us to an entire ecosystem of wings and nests and trees outside of ourselves. When watching a bird, we are completely present, immersed in a similar way to when we are composing a poem or a work of prose. Our attention remains heightened.

Last summer, after a thorny break up, and as my book tour for *Blue Atlas* drew to a close, I began to intentionally seek out new interests. I missed the physical sensation of experiencing beginner's mind. While out on the road, I was joined by my poet friend, Angie Vorhies, an avid birder who can observe the antics of a crow for an hour with intense, childlike wonder. Sometimes, walking together was very slow. However, I am thankful that a little of her bird obsession rubbed off on me.

A couple of months later, when I was ready to immerse myself in a new love, birds immediately came to mind. The idea for *Birdbrains: A Lyrical Guide to Washington State Birds* arrived all at once, whole cloth, over a long holiday weekend. On the Friday afternoon I immediately started drawing up lists of poets and writers to ask to participate. Would anyone be interested in choosing a bird to write about? Martha Silano was the first to respond asking if she could claim the Bald Eagle. Linda Bierds immediately offered her poem on "The Swifts" and Arlene Nagawana scooped the Bewick's Wren. By Saturday morning, I'd heard back from Raven Chronicles Press Managing Editor, Phoebe Bosche. She wanted to know more. Soon poets and writers were signing on with incredible alacrity—and speed. Greg November's flash fiction, "A Nest Becomes a Nest," on the Merlin falcon, arrived and soon after Derek Sheffield's poem, "To Do," on the Pileated Woodpecker. I'd asked for bird-centered poetry and prose as opposed to human-centered, 20 lines maximum. Soon, I put together a small Birdbrain curriculum teaching several poetic forms with examples from Pamela Moore Dionne, Anya Krirshbaum, and others, which was used at Seattle Children's with Ann Teplick's fabulous students (see collaborative poem inside!).

Reader, exactly one month transpired between my first idea to matchmake birds with humans—and a signed contract with Raven Chronicles Press to produce *Birdbrains: A Lyrical Guide to Washington State Birds*. If you are also a writer (or have a writer in your life) you know that a month from book concept to book contract is a near impossibility. I've authored or co-authored eight books previous to this one with the average wait to secure a publisher and sign a contract, being several years—never months, let alone one month.

In that initial four weeks between idea and the contract, I also found my two collaborators: Hiroko Seki and Stephanie Delaney; there could be no book without them. Hiroko, the visual genius of the team, was recommended to me through Connie Sidles via Birds Connect Seattle. When Hiroko and I met for the first time so that I could view her ink drawings to check if she was a good match for the project, I knew the universe was helping midwife this book. Hiroko's 100+ plein air and studio paintings are extraordinary—filled with the exact gesture and specific feeling to fit each bird.

Soon, dark-eyed juncos and swifts began appearing in my poems. I fell in love with these new words—the sounds and mysteries of altitudinal migration and magnetoreception (both words explained in the glossary). But would I ever be able to identify a bird who might look four different ways depending on their season, gender, or age? And then there's the varied songs and calls. The average Brown Thrasher knows over 1,000 different songs and 3,000 unique song phrases. The Northern Mockingbird produces between 43 to 200 tunes. What's a new bird lover to do?

Well, luckily, we are not alone. There are organizations such as the American Bird Conservancy, Birds Connect Seattle, Cornell Labs, Seattle Feminist Bird Club, and the Washington Audubon Society—all mentioned in our Resources Guide which offer classes, trips, and worlds of information.

"I am out with lanterns looking for myself," the poet, Emily Dickinson, wrote in a letter to her friend Elizabeth Holland in 1856. Maybe that's the joy of birding—looking for a piece of oneself that can naturally soar.

I confess that my heart seems to leap as the Northern Flicker perches on my feeder and we look directly into each other's eye. And although the Great Blue Heron, the Anna's Hummingbird, and the Trumpeter Swan were wildly popular with poets, no one ever asked for "my" migrating medium-sized, woodpecker. When matchmaking poets with birds for this guidebook, I confess I kept the Northern Flicker for myself. They are the only woodpeckers that migrate, offering one of the few calls I can recognize outside my window. I confess, much of my bird watching happens at my bedroom window.

However, last summer, I flew off on my first birding trip with Angie. At her suggestion, we found ourselves in the grasslands of Portugal. On this once-in-a-lifetime trip, we encountered dozens of birds that were new to me (Black Kites, Corn Buntings, and Red-rumped Swallows, for example). But what I remember, most of all, were the plethora of streetlights along the highway—each lamppost had been claimed as the foundation for a Stork's nest. There were miles of roadway, as far as one could see, exposing hundreds of lampposts that boasted nests as big around as large washbasins. In many instances, the storks were there with their young. I had the distinct impression that the birds were observing the cars zipping by underneath their makeshift condos with some interest, as if they were watching the evening news.

Yes, I believe that the birds watch us, too. You can see the moment of connection in dozens of Hiroko Seki's paintings, which she often paints plein air. I am thinking especially of her Black Oyster Catcher and Dark-eyed Junco; the House Finch and the Spotted Owl. If the birds are not looking directly out from the page, they are glancing at us sideways.

Nowadays, I walk my West Seattle neighborhood pointing out bald eagles and red-tailed hawks to friends, as well as patient strangers. My library of bird-related books insists on growing. Right now, I'm in the middle of reading Jennifer Ackerman's *The Genius of Birds* and learned last night that there are some 10,400 bird species worldwide. In this collection, *Birdbrains: A Lyrical Guide to Washington State Birds*, you will find 107 of them, many of which are global citizens. For example, the Chukar is found in Pakistan and Palestine as well as Eastern Washington; the Sandhill Crane inhabits North America and Siberia; even the Snow Geese which are so well-loved in the Skagit Valley, are only stopping over on their migration from the Arctic to winter in Mexico.

There's a saying among people who look up at the sky to view birds—the more you study birds, the smarter they become. That's the inside joke for the title of this anthology. Birdbrain is a compliment to the birds and to the humans who take time to study them. Magpies can recognize themselves in the mirror; Chickadees collect one thousand seeds a day, hide them over miles, and then find them again; and crows frequently hold crow funerals after one of their own dies— first there is stillness, then quiet, then keening. From the most common Rock Pigeon, to the rare Mystērium Rara Avis, we hope this collection will offer you wonder and joy. Get up from wherever you are sitting right now and go outdoors, binoculars or not. Watch what is happening all around us. With the right kind of attention, what might we see?

Susan Rich, Editor

CONTENTS

SHOREBIRDS

JAEGER | ALCIDS | GULLS & TERNS

SHRIKE | VIREOS | CORVIDS | SWALLOWS

CHICKADEES | BUSHTITS | NUTHATCHES | CREEPERS | WRENS | DIPPER | KINGLETS | THRUSHES

BLACKBIRDS | FINCHES | SPARROWS

STARLING | WAXWINGS | WARBLERS

NATIVE SPARROWS | WESTERN TANAGER | LAZULI BUNTING

FOREWORD

by Dr. Ursula Valdez

It has been almost 23 years since I arrived in Washington State. As an ornithologist with experience in the tropics, I was curious about the birds I would encounter in my new home. Soon, I was captivated by American Crows, Anna's Hummingbirds, Great Blue Herons, Bald Eagles, Pileated Woodpeckers, Ruby-crowned Kinglets, and many others. I've loved learning the natural history and ecology of Washington. I've also developed a strong connection with the birds here, not only because I study them, but because I love the good feelings that birds bring to my life. I am not alone in this; many people develop strong connections with birds in different ways.

And this is why I want to tell you about the book you hold in your hands, *Birdbrains: A lyrical guide to Washington State Birds*, edited by Susan Rich. It is a fantastic work of art in words and illustrations that has been inspired by the diversity of birds that live in our state. It is in fact, a lyrical guide to the life of birds, capturing through marvelous and touching poems, elements that make us curious and appreciative of these neighbors. You don't need to be an ornithologist or birdwatcher to appreciate this book; it is for bird and art lovers of all forms, who want their curious eyes, hearts, and souls filled.

I read through the pages with delight and admiration. *Birdbrains* brings to the stage 107 species of Washington birds in the words of ninety-eight talented poets and writers. The contributors come from different regions of Washington State, from other parts of the USA, and even from faraway lands such as Ireland. In the mix of talent, there are contributions from four Washington State Poet Laureates (Elizabeth Austen, Claudia Castro Luna, Kathleen Flenniken, and Derek Sheffield), three Pulitzer Prize winners (Rae Armantrout, Ted Kooser, and Diane Seuss) and a special collaborative poem by Ann Teplick's young students at Seattle Children's.

Another remarkable experience looking through the pages, is to observe the delicate lines and sketches that feature each species, in the artistic brush of Japanese artist Hiroko Seki. In page after page, the ornithologist in me is delighted to see, for example, the distinctive silhouette of a Sandhill Crane, the hunting posture of a Green Heron, the decisive dive of a Belted Kingfisher, and many more species' features, expressions, and behaviors Seki's style captures so well.

I find this creative guide heartwarming and also outstanding because the poetry and prose show not only the talent and feelings of the authors, but within them you can also see snippets that allude to the morphological, behavioral, and ecological features of the species. I read with a big smile about "the scarlet bottle rocket, that feeds upside down in a red columbine," as Anya Kirshbaum expresses so beautifully. The Anna's Hummingbird is one of my favorite species and I often watch them doing exactly this. I enjoyed Harold Taw's humor as he expressed the sassy attitude of Steller's Jays in their own language. Taw's piece captures so well, the intelligent corvid, which in real life has its own sounds to request food from accommodating humans and is also capable of imitating hawk voices which trick the most experienced birder.

In this era of division, social conflicts, and insane wars; I find my personal inspiration in nature. Birds live where they want, paying little attention to borders. I reflect on the welcoming of Chukars to eastern Washington, a species originally found in the Arab world and Asia. In her poignant poem, "Red Legs," Naomi Shihab Nye asks "Chukar, how have you come so far," marveling at the many places in the world Chukars now call home. I take note of Susan Landgraf's poem, "We're Here to Tell You," in which she alludes to a community of Black-capped Chickadees. In her memorable personal poem, Landgraff shares how the chickadees collaborate in musical voices which they use to pass on the day's information: the discovery of favorite foods from your backyard. Birds, for the most part, are collaborators—when a predator is spotted by one, the others call out.

Finally, I am thankful for the stellar job Susan Rich has done bringing together this display of human art. I appreciate that she's invited Stephanie Delaney, a dedicated birder and naturalist to contribute short notes on the birds' descriptions, habitats, as well as "interesting tidbits." With this compilation of literature, illustrations, and facts, it is remarkable to see the many ways birds can unite humans. It's the birds that allow the poets and writers here to showcase their diverse talents— collaborating across states, countries, and even continents. You just should not miss reading *Birdbrains: A Lyrical Guide to Washington State Birds*. Take this lyrical guidebook into the field, and form even stronger connections with birds and with the humans who love them.

WITH GRATITUDE

An anthology like this only comes together with the help of an entire community—or in this case, several communities. For this book of art, bird notes, and literature we are thankful to the many humans who offered us their expertise. For Susan's editorial support group, we want to thank Elizabeth Bradfield, Kristie Frederick Daugherty, and Erin Murphy. For the poets' consultancy circle: Kelli Russell Agodon, Kathleen Flenniken, and Cindy Veach. Thank you, also, to Jen McKiernan of Birds Connect Seattle who offered the key resource of Constance Sidles. We would all like to thank Constance Sidles without whom this book would not have been possible. Additionally, we are thankful to everyone at Raven Chronicles Press for believing in this project from the start.

Most of all, we appreciate you, dear reader, for taking this book into your life. Thank you for allowing us to be your guide whether you are an experienced birder or just beginning your birding journey; whether you are a lover of literature, or simply curious how a bald eagle pairs with an abecedarian. In these uncertain times, we thank everyone who cares about birds and poetry, art and science.

A FEW NOTES ABOUT THE BIRD NOTES

The notes in this book are aimed at beginning birders. Each bird note includes a brief description of the bird and where it can be found. I aimed to identify a specific Washington location in both western and eastern Washington when appropriate. The places mentioned are just one example of where the birds can be found. For far more specific details on where to find birds in all areas of the state, visit Bird Web (birdweb.org) from Birds Connect Seattle. For endangered birds, I did not include specific locations because it is best to leave those birds alone.

You will notice that I've referred to the birds as "they" and avoided "it" as birds are part of the more-than-human world; "it" usually refers to inanimate objects. This subtle shift in language serves to remind us that birds are living, breathing, beings—worthy of our attention and protection.

Finally, in the descriptions, for the most part I only described male birds. This was to keep the descriptions brief and because the male is the bird commonly described when describing a bird to beginners. Identifying females in many birds can be rather challenging for beginning birders. However, taking the time to engage in slow birding and observing female birds can be a feminist act, pushing back against the strong male bias of the bird world.

Stephanie Delaney

The Words

Wind, bird, and tree,
Water, grass, and light:
Roughly or smoothly
Year by impatient year,
The same six words recur.

I have as many floors
As meadows or rivers,
As much still air as wind
And as many cats in mind
As nests in the branches
To put an end to these.

Instead, I take what is;
The light beats on the stones,
And wind over water shines
Like long grass through the trees,
As I set loose, like birds
In a landscape, the old words.

—David Wagoner

WATERFOWL

—

DUCKS

—

GEESE

—

SWANS

BUFFLEHEAD – BUCEPHALA ALBEOLA

DESCRIPTION: North America's smallest diving duck, the Bufflehead is an eye catcher, with a black and white body and white head; their face appears iridescent green and purple in sunlight, black under clouds. With a small size and a plump body, the Bufflehead is a truly cute duck.

VOICE: Buffleheads are pretty quiet birds but are occasionally heard making a kind of clucking grunt in alarm.

HABITAT: October through May, Buffleheads are quite common in fresh and saltwater areas of all sizes, even tiny ponds where they eat aquatic insects, crustaceans, and mollusks.

INTRIGUING TIDBIT: The Bufflehead returns to the same mate for many years. They use old Northern Flicker nests to raise their young.

DATE AND LOCATION SEEN:

Thirteen Seconds in Heaven

Bring me under, completely

Under with you, to forage for waterlogged

Food—snails, crustaceans, insects, plants—

For just thirteen seconds at a time, on constant repeat.

Let me eat, eat, eat all day like this, insatiable,

Elemental duck.

Hunger, submerged.

Eccentricity, my colors necklaced.

Around my sworn-to-secret underwater ravagings, my

Ducky feathered, larger-than-life bufflehead.

—Sandra Yannone

COMMON GOLDENEYE – BUCEPHALA CLANGULA

DESCRIPTION: The Common Goldeneye is a medium-sized diving duck with bright yellow, or golden, eyes. This winter migrant is often seen in November through April in small flocks, or in ones and twos.

VOICE: The sound most connected with the Goldeneye is the clear, loud whistle which emits from the wings of the male in flight.

HABITAT: The Goldeneye enjoys protected salt water and freshwater lakes where they dive for food—eating clams, crabs, and other invertebrates. Also, look for them in winter months on the Snake and Columbia Rivers.

INTRIGUING TIDBIT: The male Goldeneye puts on a distinctive and humorous courtship display where males dramatically throw their heads back and emit a loud call.

DATE AND LOCATION SEEN:

The Whistlers

It's not how they forage as a flock, or how
the drake's head can gleam green in sunlight.

It's not the fourteen moves a drake makes
to impress a hen or how hens never hesitate

to roost in another hen's nest.
It's not their late migration south in dreary

November from the terrain of boreal trees,
and not even the uncommon radiant amber eyes.

No, their specialty is a nine beat-per-second
song they make when flying, a drumroll thrum

of echo off water, this whistle from down and bone
rolling across the sea. If you hear it

you may turn and watch to see a flock
of ducks just landing, skimming water, webbed feet

straining to touch, wings outstretched to slow
and quiet in this wild numinous.

—Cheryl Waitkevich

CANADA GOOSE – BRANTA CANADENSIS

DESCRIPTION: The Canada Goose is a large brown waterfowl, easily identifiable and exceptionally common. They have a long black neck, head, and bill, with a bold white cheek patch. They are social birds that mate for life, maintaining strong family ties.

VOICE: You can hear a wide variety of sounds from Canada Geese, from honks and hissing to low clucks and murmurs.

HABITAT: Canada Geese like grassy fields, parks, golf courses, and other areas with manicured lawns where they can both find food and keep an eye out for predators. You can find them year-round in Washington in urban settings like Seattle's Green Lake Park or more natural areas like the Nisqually National Wildlife Refuge.

INTRIGUING TIDBIT: Goslings begin communicating with their parents while still in the egg.

DATE AND LOCATION SEEN:

Dear Canada Goose,

You are the original silly goose. Swan-shaped without the grace. Honking walnut-brained bread solicitor. Black-necked and black-headed aggressively pecking for bread. When I lived with her, my grandmother would take me to Wallace Pond and bring heels of bread loaves. I fed you until I realized I was only feeding your aggression.

Your name has never made sense to me. Nothing winged has a nationality. Creatures are not tied to the arbitrary borders of where they were born.

I find a range map indicating you breed in Canada. A button on the page reads *Learn more at Birds of the World* but I misread it as *Learn more about the birds at the end of the world.* Is that how you feel in flight? When you migrate, are you fleeing or fighting? I too am a living heterotopia, unable to be pinned to one country, identity, culture. Has anyone asked you, *Where are you from? No, where are you really from?* Have you ever answered? I look to the sky, and sometimes, when I look long enough, I turn blue and vanish.

—Mateo Acuña-Bracken

CINNAMON TEAL – ANAS CYANOPTERA

DESCRIPTION: The Cinnamon Teal is a striking duck, sporting a rich cinnamon-colored plumage, a blue bill, and a red eye. Male Cinnamon Teals attract the plain brown females with a series of rapid head bobs and neck stretches.

VOICE: The Cinnamon Teal is not often heard. Males have a chattering call during courtship and females may quack in alarm.

HABITAT: Spring through fall, you can find the Cinnamon Teal in shallow ponds and marshes in places like the Lower Columbia River or in urban areas like the Union Bay Natural Area in Seattle. They are dabbling ducks that eat aquatic plants and small invertebrates.

INTRIGUING TIDBIT: When nesting, Cinnamon Teals will fake a wing injury to lure predators away from their young.

DATE AND LOCATION SEEN:

Mother Ship

In the pond,
a female Cinnamon Teal paddles with her babies,
mother ship followed by seven little tugboats,
fueled with green algae.

—Constance Sidles

COMMON MERGANSER – MERGUS MERGANSER

DESCRIPTION: The Common Merganser is a large duck with a long thin serrated bill. Males are mostly white with a dark green head and females have a cinnamon head and white chin. They swim low in the water and dive for their food.

VOICE: Common Mergansers are generally quiet birds, that may vocalize with a hoarse croaking sound during courtship.

HABITAT: You'll find Common Mergansers in clear, freshwater habitats including lakes, rivers, reservoirs, and, in winter, coastal areas. They like wooded areas as the females nest, often communally, in trees.

INTRIGUING TIDBIT: Common Mergansers may swim with their heads underwater searching for fish. They can remain underwater for up to 2 minutes.

DATE AND LOCATION SEEN:

Mergansers in the Narrow Valley of Merging Rivers

Bees hum in ground nests but do not
swarm in the settlement of soft grasses.

Sun pulling a balm from the waxy buds
of rose hips. Cottonwood parachutes cloud

the ground into a pale mat where the raging river
toes into a wide pavilion of water. Goosegrass paints

the salmon nursery a delicate shade and here at least,
in the first joining of waters are redds of protection

under the flooded roots. Even inveterate insomniacs
might flip over just once and fall asleep with the corners

of their mouths upturned on sheets bought with grocery
tickets under the tender and pastoral scent of the last

generation's ribbon star quilts. Bright orange lifejackets
hang on the tree limbs for anyone's use, bright orange

raft of crowns as the merganser hens hunt the logjam.
The Tualco Grange holds an approximate translation

for the Lushootseed word for this joining of rivers.
The penciled price on the inner cover of a paperback

at the thrift shop holds the initials of a best friend
from 8th grade. Bridges to the south and east

are a milky blue, beautiful in their stodgy authority
and bolted lines, like a bone slice under a microscope.

At the second joining, merganser heads flash emerald
bulbs of density before diving under the velvet table

of slough where willows dip their tips into the water
like a young child washing the ends of her braids.

—Laura Da'

HARLEQUIN DUCK – HISTRIONICUS HISTRIONICUS

DESCRIPTION: The Harlequin Duck is a compact bird that cannot be mistaken for any other duck. They are dark blue with chestnut sides and crown, and have striking white markings on the face, neck, sides, and back.

VOICE: Fairly vocal for a sea duck, the Harlequin Duck makes a consistent, yapping call.

HABITAT: Harlequin Ducks are found along rocky coastlines, preferably with rough surf. Look for them in winter in places like the Semiahmoo Spit. In summer, they retreat to the mountains to breed in fast moving mountain streams.

INTRIGUING TIDBIT: Because of their preference for rough water, especially in the breeding season, many Harlequin Ducks have been found with broken bones, likely from being dashed against rough rocks.

DATE AND LOCATION SEEN:

Ode to the Harlequin Duck

My dear *histrionicus histrionicus*, your name
means actor, means drama, means something
over the top. Oh wingèd warrior, you choose
the roughest water, rocks pounding
the surf, pounding you, sometimes breaking
your bones, yet you boys have the coolest
dance moves, tail raised, neck stretched, always
the court jester, bobbing your head
so we have to consider that unmistakable
face. Even your migration is weird, east-west
instead of north-south like other ducks, and I love
how you swim and wing your way against the current,
following each bend of the river, flying low,
never just taking the easy way home.

—KateLynn Hibbard

MALLARD – ANAS PLATYRHYNCHOS

DESCRIPTION: From their iridescent green heads and bright yellow bills to their curly-cue black tail feathers, the Mallard is a quintessential duck. Indeed, they are the most widespread duck in Washington State and the most common duck in North America. A large dabbling duck, they have gray bodies and chestnut chests under a white neck ring, and orange legs and feet.

VOICE: The familiar "quack, quack" of the Mallard is made primarily by the female ducks.

HABITAT: The Mallard is highly adaptable and is found nearly everywhere there is open water including urban and suburban areas. You can find them year-round in marshes, low water wetlands, and places like the Skagit River Valley where they breed all the way to Ross Lake. They are highly social birds, often found in mated pairs or larger groups.

INTRIGUING TIDBIT: Mallards frequently interbreed with closely related species and have hybridized with more than 40 species in the wild. If you see a strange duck in a city park, it may well be a type of Mallard.

DATE AND LOCATION SEEN:

Leaving

The sheen of the drake's, bright
green against the pond's water,
reflects up against its throat
so that, the green is mirrored there,
in his slickened breast, the sun
twinning the bird so he is twice
iridescent in the rebound of light
off water and he lifts himself, not quite
in flight, but alight, patterned
and dappled with blue streaks
flashing forward beneath his wings
which were once tucked under, but
now shook blue and blue and strange,
with water parting from his plumage
in an arc from his wingbeat pitched
so that he rises now, above
where his reflection also lingers,
framed by the concentric circles
of pond splash and then smaller
and smaller still as the mallard
who was once still, stills
the pond with his leaving.

—Oliver de la Paz

NORTHERN SHOVELER – SPATULA CLYPEATA

DESCRIPTION: Northern Shovelers are medium-sized dabbling ducks with large shovel-shaped bills that give them their name. They have iridescent green heads, white chests, and chestnut-colored bellies and sides. Also, they boast orange-yellow legs and feet. They are social birds, often seen in small flocks. You may see them swimming in circles with their bills submerged, sweeping from side to side, filtering tiny aquatic insects from the water.

VOICE: A relatively quiet duck, male Northern Shovelers make a low clunking call and females a light Mallard-like quack.

HABITAT: Northern Shovelers prefer shallow wetlands, marshes and ponds, all with abundant vegetation. In winter they also visit coastal marshes, estuaries, flooded fields, and wastewater ponds. Look for them throughout the state in August through May, in places like the Ridgefield National Wildlife Refuge or Green Lake in Seattle.

INTRIGUING TIDBIT: Female Northern Shovelers will defend their eggs from predators by defecating on them before flushing away to deter the threat.

DATE AND LOCATION SEEN:

Kiss Me Like a Shoveler...

After seeing a limpkin go at
a snail we joke, *Kiss me like
a limpkin.* Meaning really get
in there and go for the meat. Or
like an avocet—chin swept
across my shoulder's skin, bill
slightly parted. Don't kiss me
like a heron, quick, hard stab
and retreat. Or like a turkey
(random pecks). I'd take it
like a sanderling, though,
stippling the shoreline
of my thigh. And, yes,
yes! Like a shoveler.
Your wide, particular
mouthbill, tight as a coin
purse until you seek to satisfy
your hunger and then, agape,
seeking together, aswirl, we help
each other get what we want,
circling to spin up what will
gratify. Kiss me like a shoveler
in an ecstasy of shovelers,
all of us one big pinwheel now,
a rave, water rippling out
from our twirl, from the serious
business of our mouths, free
of any self-consciousness,
focused on satisfaction, light
gleaming on the lustrous
black-green or soft chinchilla
of the backs of our bent
and intent heads.

—Elizabeth Bradfield

RING-NECKED DUCK – AYTHYA COLLARIS

DESCRIPTION: The Ring-necked Duck is a medium-sized diving duck, black with gray sides and a peaked head. You're more likely to notice the ring at the tip of their gray bill than at their necks, as the ring on their necks is rarely visible.

VOICE: Ring-necked Ducks are mostly quiet, though the males may make a whistling call.

HABITAT: You're more likely to find Ring-necked Ducks on small, shallow, tree-lined ponds and lakes. They like to hide in vegetation at night rather than stay out in the open. More common in the winter, you can find them September through March in places like Meadowbrook Pond in Seattle.

INTRIGUING TIDBIT: Unlike other ducks, Ring-necked Ducks can leap straight from the water into flight, rather than having to get a running start. Thus, they are not hampered by small ponds surrounded by trees.

DATE AND LOCATION SEEN:

Every Other Duck on the Pond

Maybe in a crowd
of dabblers, you dive. Or when
all the other divers struggle—
a long hard take-off—
from the water's rise and fall, you burst
straight up. To stand out,
that's fine.

But what if you hide,
like the ring-necked duck,
a cinnamon ribbon
in the folds of your feathers?
In every dip or swallow, you alone
know the glorious. You alone
slide over the blue, certain
that you matter.

—Deborah Bacharach

SNOW GOOSE – ANSER CAERULESCENS

DESCRIPTION: The Snow Goose is a large white goose with black wingtips that can be seen clearly during flight. They have compact pink bills and orange legs. They can be seen hanging out in very large flocks of thousands of birds.

VOICE: The high-pitched, barking call of the Snow Goose is a nasal single syllable honk. Snow Geese are the most vocal of all waterfowl.

HABITAT: From mid-October to early May, you can find the Snow Goose in coastal and freshwater marshes, estuaries, and agricultural lands like those in the Ridgefield National Wildlife Refuge or the Skagit Valley. Up to 55,000 Snow Geese a year make the Skagit River Delta their winter home, where they dine on aquatic insects and plants.

INTRIGUING TIDBIT: The breeding grounds for Snow Geese are in the Arctic tundra. The ones seen in Washington come from Wrangel Island, Siberia.

DATE AND LOCATION SEEN:

Snow Geese

almost always migrate. Their spectacular aerial show
blots out the skies with thousands of birds—
communities of siblings, fathers & mothers—
doing what this waterfowl naturally do
embarking en masse from Mexico & the U.S. to
feed on arctic plants & roots. To make goslings. To
grow their kin & kind. Behold their rhythmic
honk & squawk. Marvel at their
immense formation, & their steady, steady wingbeat.

Just ten years ago, *The Snow Goose Cookbook*
kindly urged us to eat our way out of this
large & growing species, by making goose croquettes in the name of
managing arctic habitats. The bird's gamey tough meat
notwithstanding. But I refuse to eat you, Beloved.
Or to complain about your greenish
poop that carpets the Skagit Delta. Oh,
Quintessential Sign of the Passing of Seasons. Oh,
Regal Pilgrim of the Open Water. Never
stop multiplying. Your abundant life in
the present eco-disaster inspires. Be
unwavering, be millions, be our future. When the earth's
very existence is unknown, spread your black-tipped
winged plumage like a prayer. Pray for our
xenogenesis from destructive inheritance: for
yellow offspring with bright eyes
zig-zagging towards soft new grass.

—Renee E. Simms

TRUMPETER SWAN – CYGNUS BUCCINATOR

DESCRIPTION: The largest waterfowl in North America, the Trumpeter Swan is a white bird with a long neck and a black bill. It is a convivial bird that mates for life.

VOICE: The Trumpeter Swan gets its name from its voice—low, nasal, single notes that remind one of a toy trumpet.

HABITAT: The Trumpeter Swan can be found in lakes, ponds, agricultural fields, and coastal bays in places like Whatcom and Snohomish counties. They dine on aquatic plants, waste grain, and potatoes. This winter migrant is often found in flocks in the winter.

INTRIGUING TIDBIT: Hunting nearly drove the Trumpeter Swan to extinction in Washington State 50 years ago, but conservation efforts have supported them in making a comeback.

DATE AND LOCATION SEEN:

The Swans of Shadow Lake

On Shadow Lake, a bevy of swans dream
    within a field of stars, one leg dangling
beneath each, as if cast at anchor, their young
    clustered round them as they dream
themselves a flight, though their bodies, largest
    of native birds in North America, drift
on a silver film of moonlight.
                                  One is grieving.
    The cob plunges its beak into the oval
of the moon sliding over the surface of the lake,
where the bird once fed with its paired lover
    from tubers of pondweed, rushes and sedges,
and the swan, alone now, recalls years of nesting,
    feeding, the long migrations north and south,
and how, this past spring, his lover grew frail,
    as pellets of lead ground in the gizzard
and ingested, absorbed in the pen's bloodstream,
    her muscles growing weaker, until she could
no longer fly, her great wings opening and closing,
though no longer lifting her on the invisible,
    the ocean of air no longer her home.
There is nothing left now but the raising of cygnets,
    to see their young rise into the dawn itself,
their bodies turning gold then blue then gone forever,
    the way it is for us all. And the cob, still grieving,
uncurls its slender neck from the question of its body,
    that it might spread its wings ten feet wide,

that it might call out to its lover—no matter
the silent repose of trees, no matter the echo
   of that stillness on the surface of the lake.
                   Is it all so strange?
The swan grieves in a manner wholly true
   to the kingdom of flight, and yet
is it not unlike the signature cry
   of the human heart, emptied of the world?

          —Brian Turner

WOOD DUCK – AIX SPONSA

DESCRIPTION: The Wood Duck is a striking bird with green, purple, bronze and white plumage. They are a medium-sized dabbling duck. Their head feathers form a helmet shape and they have red eyes. Sharp nails on their webbed feet allow them to perch in trees, an unusual trait in a duck.

VOICE: Unlike most ducks, Wood Ducks don't quack. Rather, the males make a high pitched whistle and the females make a squeal that sounds like "oooeeek."

HABITAT: Wood Ducks nest in trees or nest boxes and they prefer habitats near ponds, swamps, or slow-moving streams near trees and dense vegetation. Look for Wood Ducks during the summer months in places like the Montlake Fill in Seattle.

INTRIGUING TIDBIT: Baby Wood Ducks are expected to leap from their tree nests, as high as 60 feet, just a day after hatching. They never return to the nest.

DATE AND LOCATION SEEN:

Wood Duck at Wapato Park, Showing Out

Touch the water, summer bird,
Touch the water, then strut
your wings as in devotion.
Tell us, in your high tenor
of home and it's specifics
that we mimeograph in block
           after block.

Take your wings and show your color(s)
—your Burgundys—your Blues
—your heavy dirt clay tones that make
           us yearn
for a journey back (if only for a time).
Validate the now if not the memory
of woods free from the remembrance of blood,
of grass free from bones, and mobless parks
and seven seals unbroken from sturdy branches,
then flash the neon iridsesence you hide
in the cold. You among your people now.
Testify in the water, oh colored southern bird
Testify on your portable promised lands.

—Robert Lashley

GALLINACEOUS BIRDS

—

LOONS

—

GREBES

—

CORMORANTS

—

PELICANS

—

HERONS

AMERICAN WHITE PELICAN – PELECANUS ERYTHRORHYNCHOS

DESCRIPTION: The American White Pelican is one of the nation's largest birds, measuring 50–70 inches and sporting a wingspan of 8 to 10 feet. They are white with black wingtips, yellow legs and feet, and an orange bill with the distinctive pelican throat pouch. Despite their large size, the American White Pelican is a highly efficient, powerful, and graceful flier, soaring on thermal currents and taking advantage of V-shaped flight formations. This efficiency allows them to migrate very long distances.

VOICE: You will rarely hear this quiet bird. When they do vocalize, the American White Pelican makes low grunts or croaks.

HABITAT: Primarily an inland bird, the American White Pelican can be found on Washington's large, inland freshwater lakes as well as areas like the Columbia Plateau. They also visit Whidbey Island every year. They migrate to warmer coastal areas in the winter.

INTRIGUING TIDBIT: American White Pelicans do not dive for fish. Rather, they form cooperative hunting teams to herd fish together and then scoop them up.

DATE AND LOCATION SEEN:

Spreading Ashes

My father flew on a white pelican
into the sky when the sails
of his boat no longer unfurled
and the lakebed ran dry

the pelican scooped him up
into the squadron, carried
his ashes from Oregon
to the Columbia, to Walla Walla

and then, turning west, soared
(though some would say I imagined it)
to the shore of the Salish
Sea where I saw this white pelican

skim the pearling water. My father
glided off the creche of the pelican's
black-tipped back, bringing
his bones back to me.

–Sarah Stockton

BROWN PELICAN – PELECANUS OCCIDENTALIS CALIFORNICUS

DESCRIPTION: Brown Pelicans are large sea birds with grayish-brown bodies and a white head and neck. They have a distinctive long beak with a thin pouch that they use to scoop up fish when diving from heights of up to 30 feet.

VOICE: Generally quiet, the Brown Pelican may make grunting sounds during the breeding season or when defending themselves.

HABITAT: You'll find Brown Pelicans in coastal waters, estuaries, and bays. They are most often seen May through November in places like the Columbia River Estuary, Grays Harbor, or Willapa Bay. Brown Pelicans are social birds, often travelling in squadrons and roosting communally.

INTRIGUING TIDBIT: Brown Pelicans are one of the few pelicans to plunge dive for their food. The others simply scoop the fish up.

DATE AND LOCATION SEEN:

Footprints Erased with Each Wave

Because your wife died, you wanted
to see the ocean.

We crested small dunes, shadows
ghosting us.

Lifting hands to shield
squinted eyes,

we saw,
backlit,

the elegant pattern of bones
inside a pelican's spread wings

held nearly still
on the updraft,

wings folded whip quick,
head tucked left

so the body could
plunge fast

fast behind breaking surf
then reassemble itself

like a man in deep grief
letting everything he can

drain away, every breath
drain away—

—Peggy Shumaker

BLACK-CROWNED NIGHT HERON – NYCTICORAX NYCTICORAX

DESCRIPTION: The Black-crowned Night Heron is a medium-sized, stocky heron with a black cap and back and large red eyes over a sharp black bill. They have short yellow legs.

VOICE: The call of the Black-crowned Night Heron is a loud "kwok," often made at dusk or at night.

HABITAT: Night Herons can be found in marshes and wetlands and the shores of rivers, lakes and ponds. Look for them year round in the Columbia Basin. As their name suggests, they are primarily a nocturnal bird, becoming active at dusk hunting fish, amphibians, and invertebrates in shallow water. They roost in groups during the day in trees near the water.

INTRIGUING TIDBIT: Populations of the Black-crowned Night Heron are declining across their range, including Washington. This is due to habitat loss, water pollution, and human disturbance. They are also subject to competition from Double-crested Cormorants for preferred nesting sites.

DATE AND LOCATION SEEN:

Remembering the Black-Crowned Night Heron

Years ago, before I ended my long marriage,
I saw a bird, hunched, a bird unknown to me,
near the creek in our front yard. I saw it catch
and swallow a snake which tried to escape
but the bird insisted and gulp by gulp inched the prey
down its throat. Stocky, broody, a heron without the allure
of the long-legged, long necked Great Blue. A heron
whose call is a bark, whose bill crushes a crustacean
in seconds. A bird who'll care for anyone's chicks,
who is dominated by other herons and egrets in the day
and hunts at night with light-gathering red eyes.
I see you high up on a branch waiting for nightfall.
I see you *still fishing* at the water's edge, patient, persistent.
With one lightning-quick thrust of your beak you sever
a crab's pincers, take what you need without apology.

—Cindy Veach

CALIFORNIA QUAIL – CALLIPEPLA CALIFORNICA

DESCRIPTION: Sporting a bobbing yet elegant top knot, the California Quail is a distinctive small plump brownish bird with a short tail and a face with white stripes. The California Quail is known for gathering year-round in large coveys of 20 or more. It also has large clutches of up to 20 eggs.

VOICE: These quails make a series of soft, musical calls that some hear as "Chi-ca-go." They also make a staccato "pit-pit-pit-pit" call that helps the coveys stay together.

HABITAT: You'll find the coveys in open areas surrounded by dense brush, allowing them to forage to find seeds and run for cover when needed. Look for these birds in places like the Sequim-Dungeness Prairies.

INTRIGUING TIDBIT: Coveys of California Quail will post a male guard on high ground to watch for predators and warn of danger.

DATE AND LOCATION SEEN:

Quail Without a Covey

Every day he paces the deck railing
being sociable with his reflection in the windows.

His old covey wandered off in a wobbly line
so he's trying to break in with this new one

garbed in gray and brown graduation gowns
and jaunty black bullion tassels.

They're handsome but standoffish.
What will become of him

with no appetite for seeds or leaves
or even a pleasant dirt bath—

only worry and trying to look casual
and the need to belong.

I feel it too on the dark side of the glass.

—Kathleen Flenniken

COMMON LOON – GAVIA IMMER

DESCRIPTION: Common Loons are Washington's largest water bird by weight. During the fall through spring non-breeding season, the time they are typically seen in Washington, they have a grayish-brown plumage, red eyes, and a strong, pointed bill. In breeding season, their plumage is a striking black and white including a checkered black and white pattern on their backs and white patterned color at the neck.

VOICE: The Common Loon has a haunting, 3-part wail.

HABITAT: Common Loons prefer large, clear lakes and coastal habitats where they can catch small fish by sight. Because they are so heavy, they need long stretches of open water to take off for flight. Their legs, placed far back on their bodies, cause them to swim exceptionally well but walk awkwardly.

INTRIGUING TIDBIT: The Common Loon's wailing call can sound like wild laughter, leading to the phrase "crazy as a loon."

DATE AND LOCATION SEEN:

Psalm of the Loon

Did you hear him calling along the blue morning?
His throat filled with sorrow on the lake?
Tears falling from carnelian eyes?
Did you see the thrash, a froth of waves,
before he dove, in search of her still?

He arches his neck, lifts his dark head,
a sip of deep water in his sharp black beak.
His wings open. He calls, the sound
shimmers in the air, leaves a residue.
Regret. A vast grief that mutes him.
He lifts off as shadow, as a relic mist.
Do you see sparks on the water? Reflected
sunlight? Candles lit for a mass of the dead?
Can you see her, unmoving, just below?

—Pamela Moore Dionne

DOUBLE-CRESTED CORMORANT – PHALACROCORAX AURITUS

DESCRIPTION: The Double-crested Cormorant is a large black water bird with blue eyes, a yellow-orange bill, and a yellow chin area. They are very social birds, and you often find them in large colonies, for example on Protection Island.

VOICE: Generally silent, the Double-crested Cormorant may give croaks or grunts within their colonies.

HABITAT: You'll find the Double-crested Cormorant year-round in almost any aquatic area, as they are highly adaptable. They are the only cormorant that you'll find in inland areas. Look for them in coastal areas, lakes, swamps with perches for resting and drying off—as they are favorite locations for these excellent divers. They swim underwater to catch bottom fish, holding their wings at their sides.

INTRIGUING TIDBIT: Double-crested Cormorants are often seen perched on rocks or pilings with their wings held out, gazing up to the sky. This is to dry their outer feathers, which have less preen oil than other birds.

DATE AND LOCATION SEEN:

Warriors of the Storm

Pelagic cormorants'
wings kited out in wind
twisted in thistle-sized rain.
Bunched on summer rafts
these warriors of winter
are servile to the sea.
Their bodies evolved
to keep up with this
catnip weather
       feet clinch on ferry pilings,
       heughs heightened to elude prey,
       slickened plumage to resist the
       angry rain hissing on pilings.

—C. Hunter Davis

GREAT BLUE HERON – ARDEA HERODIAS

DESCRIPTION: Often seen patiently standing motionless in shallow waters, the Great Blue Heron convinces one that dinosaurs really did exist. The large bird's long, thin legs, snakelike neck, and lethally-sharp pointed bill give it a unique silhouette. The Great Blue Heron has a blue-gray plumage and white head with a distinct black plumage at the back of the head.

VOICE: With a harsh, guttural squawk, Great Blue Herons sound as prehistoric as they look.

HABITAT: The Great Blue Heron is found year-round in wetland habitats, rivers, lakes, and wherever they can capture fish and frogs. They are also found in open fields where they dine on small mammals and even other birds. With their massive 6-foot wingspan, it can be startling to see them land lightly in a tree, where herons nest communally. Look for them nesting at the Ballard Locks in Seattle.

INTRIGUING TIDBIT: Despite their large bodies, Great Blue Herons only weigh about 5–6 pounds due to their hollow bones, which aid flight and buoyancy.

DATE AND LOCATION SEEN:

Early Morning Song for a Great Blue Heron

Praise the Great Blue Heron,
sister of waterfall and cedar, brother of peace

Praise the great blue bird who balances,
his house, body and soul, on slender legs like homes
on stilts in fishing villages across the world

Praise the stately bearing of a blue heron carrying on
in an estuary as light succumbs to the abyss of night

Praise the Great Blue Heron's plumage, albus and umbra,
love and loathing, traces of the imperfect in the present tense

Praise the taut line between grace and gaucheness
that a Great Blue Heron traverses all the days of her life

Praise be to the noble heron witnessing
the names of the dead floating on by and by

Praise the heron's patience, humility's twin virtue,
fishing on at dusk through the murk

Praise the Great Blue Heron's ingenuity
to meet its hunger, with extended wings creating
her own weather, casting shade on quiet waters,
luring aquatic creatures for lunch

Praise the frogs and minnows, the reeds and marsh,
the wind and tides that nurture herons

This early dawn I praise the solitary Great Blue Heron,
wings folded over its body, neck tucked,
as if it is feeling the weight of the world's sorrows

Praise a Great Blue Heron in flight,
crossing sky, archer and arrow of its destiny

Praise the heron's long beak for making evident
the delight of kissing with a human mouth

Praise the great blue's loyalty to mate and place,
each year returning to the same nest

Praise the herons who after decades
decide not to return to the old nest,
and those who make room to face their many deaths
and each time let new light rush into their blue hearts

I, a Homo sapiens, praise the Great Blue Heron,
Ardea herodias, its birdiness, against which
my flawed humanity comes to light.

—Claudia Castro Luna

GREEN HERON – BUTORIDES VIRESCENS

DESCRIPTION: The Green Heron is a crow-sized, stocky heron with yellow eyes, a black cap, and a long sharp bill. They sport a dark-green iridescent back and chestnut neck, chest, and belly, over yellow legs.

VOICE: Green Herons have a sharp call that sounds like "kyow."

HABITAT: Green Herons prefer to keep a low profile in wetland habitats with dense vegetation including swamps, marshes, ponds, and streams. Between May and September, you might find this secretive bird at the Nisqually National Wildlife Refuge or Seattle's Union Bay Natural Area.

INTRIGUING TIDBIT: Few birds use tools, but the Green Heron is one of them, using bait to attract fish. They prefer to perch above the water for food rather than wade. They are also able to hover briefly to catch food, which is unusual for a heron.

DATE AND LOCATION SEEN:

Pair of Greens

Vampirish in dark capes, they stalk
damselflies at wetland's edge

and hunt from clumps of sedge
or stumps for higher ground

on account of their stout build
and hunched posture on twig legs.

Not egrets or bitterns, more sarcastic.
Not regal like their blue cousins

though juveniles don a splash of sun,
splotches on subdued plumage.

Better light reveals rainforest-
green backs, chanterelle-brown necks

and breasts, and slate-gray wings,
which on takeoff unfold akimbo.

Mid-flight, their necks might appear
unwieldy, though on the ground

Green Herons stalk smooth as a pop-
star's moonwalk.

They let us get close
staying focused on the next meal.

On each side of a claw-like beak,
a little sunstone eye—

in that fierce glare at the dragonfly,
you might recognize, a hint of pterodactyl.

—Scot Siegel

WESTERN GREBE – AECHMOPHORUS OCCIDENTALIS

DESCRIPTION: Western Grebes are water birds with long, slender, swan-like necks. They have black caps that extend below their deep red eyes and the base of their long, sharp yellow bills. The black coloring extends down the back of the neck and back while their throats and chests are white. They are social birds that nest in colonies and winter in flocks.

VOICE: The song of the Western Grebe is a rolling "krik-kreek" that sounds a bit like a cricket.

HABITAT: Western Grebes live in large fresh water lakes in the summer and also expand to sheltered bays and estuaries in the winter. Look for them breeding in places like Moses Lake.

INTRIGUING TIDBIT: The chicks of the Western Grebe climb onto their parents' backs within a few minutes of hatching and may continue to ride there for the first three to four weeks of life.

DATE AND LOCATION SEEN:

Mating Display

The cove today offers rain
and Western grebes, water-logged trunk

of a downed fir, cat-tails, hawthorn.
The grebes are dressed

in their mating-season finest,
bright feathers against the gray weather,

their bright red-rimmed eyes
like berries. Forty years back,

another rainy day in early spring,
a new boyfriend took me to see grebes.

They barge, he said. *They walk on water!*
Oh, Jesus, I thought, this guy is nuts.

Then I saw the grebes: their elegant
white throats, black top-knots like Elvis,

the Elvis dip and flirt of them,
before they got up as if on tippy-

toe and charged (barging!)
across the rain-pocked water,

chests flung out, chortling *cree, cree*.
My affair with birds began

that day. As for the boyfriend, ditto.

—Bethany Reid

VULTURES

—

EAGLES & HAWKS

—

RAILS

—

COOTS

—

CRANES

AMERICAN COOT – FULICA AMERICANA

DESCRIPTION: The American Coot is a medium-sized black water bird with a white beak and forehead. They have a reddish brown spot between their red eyes. They have long slim toes instead of webbed feet like other seabirds. Watch for their amusing head bob as they swim.

VOICE: Listen for a repeated croaking sound from the American Coot.

HABITAT: Coots prefer freshwater lakes and ponds where they can dine on insects and aquatic plants. While mostly around September through March, they can be found year-round in some areas of the Puget Sound. Look for them in huge flocks in places like Lake Washington's Union Bay or in the Columbia River Estuary.

INTRIGUING TIDBIT: American Coots can be guilty of "kleptoparasitism," stealing food from other birds in opportunistic feeding behavior. But perhaps turnabout is fair play—Coots are also the victim of theft by Wigeons who wait for diving Coots to surface with tasty water plants that the Wigeons grab.

DATE AND LOCATION SEEN:

[*fulica americana*: do you turn your head towards or against this critical mass we are a part of?]

i had almost forgotten   belonging transcends

the rocky foreground   the shoreline, water picture still

against Lake Washington.   my small human
sapience

what binary the news online   tells me who and how

i should oppose.   what moves several thousand coots
                                        closer to the center

divisible only by   the landscape? tip up their mouths,
                                        full of lake-bottom

                again & again & again—

a mass mobilization, hope   sedges, cattails water
                                    lodged with dragonflies.

pattering open ground, across water, together,   coots lift
                                                        as one
                                            airborned mass.

—Jasminé Elizabeth Smith

BALD EAGLE – HALIAEETUS LEUCOCEPHALUS

DESCRIPTION: An iconic bird, the American Eagle was nearly driven to extinction. But the Bald Eagle has made a remarkable comeback, coming off the Endangered Species list in 2007. Today you can regularly see this large bird of prey soaring with broad dark wings, white head and tail, yellow beak, and large yellow talons.

VOICE: The commanding screech that is often associated in movies and TV with the Bald Eagle is actually the voice of the Red-Tailed Hawk. The cry of the Bald Eagle is a high-pitched sound more like a chirp than the cry of the Red-Tailed Hawk.

HABITAT: The Bald Eagle is found year-round in high trees or soaring high in the sky, generally seen near water so they can swoop down and catch fresh fish or water birds. Look for them in the Upper Skagit River Valley or Gene Coulon Park in Renton.

INTRIGUING TIDBIT: Bald Eagles return to their nests year after year, adding to them each year. Indeed, they build the largest nest of any bird, sometimes weighing over 2,000 pounds.

DATE AND LOCATION SEEN:

The Bald Eagles of Seward Park

always surprise me, always make me
believe trying to fix a mistake is worth it.
Case in point: DDT, an insecticide used to eradicate

diseases like malaria and typhus.
Eradicating mosquitoes because, well,
first and foremost: the health and safety of people.

God forbid a human should've known
how this chemical would weaken the eggshells of eagles,
inching down the number in the lower 48 from 100,000 to

just 417. Yes, they harass ospreys, steal their prey, so it
kinda makes sense Ben Franklin said *He does not get his*
Living honestly, preferred, for our national bird, the wild
    turkey, but

mating for life – what's not to like? Google *Eagles and DDT*, find
NO adverse effects on humans, domestic animals, or wildlife—
    really?
Opinions graciously accepted. Free speech, I guess, which
    proliferates,

propagates like these eagles, where on a good day I
question how there could be so much chattering and pealing,
roosting and gliding. That there would be so many juveniles

soaring over the water, diving down to nab a perch.
Talon-grabbing and tumbling while mating. Cloacal kissing.
Utterly promising, isn't it? A success story! What was alarming

very much less dire now. That we banned it.
Wailed and moaned *no, no, no*. That the EPA prevented
X-ing out a regal raptor that's been around a million years, its

(yowzers) reptilian past. Stopped the slide from abundantly
     robust to
zero. That we might restore tall grass prairies, save the bees
     that feed us.

—Martha Silano

COOPER'S HAWK – ACCIPITER COOPERII

DESCRIPTION: The Cooper's Hawk is a medium-sized raptor with a flat head and red eyes. They have a blue-gray cap, back, and relatively stubby wings. Their chests are white with rusty bars. Their long blue-gray tails have three black bars.

VOICE: Cooper's Hawks are mostly silent. During the breeding season they have a loud "kak-kak-kak" call.

HABITAT: Cooper's Hawks prefer woodlands, but they can also thrive in urban areas. Look for them at forest edges and suburban landscapes perched and watching for prey.

INTRIGUING TIDBIT: William Cooper was a naturalist who collected the specimens used to describe the bird that was later named the Cooper's Hawk. He was known for advancing the field of natural history in America in the 19th Century.

DATE AND LOCATION SEEN:

Homecoming

Walking home from a party
in summer dusk
I am always walking home
from a party, the darkly lit
staircases of the clouds
sweeping upwards,
the quiet streets,
and in the park, a Cooper's hawk
perched on a branch,
pinning down the carcass
of a smaller bird with her talons.
She stands on her meal,
flaying it into strings: someone
excavating life
out of disillusionment.
A few plucked petals of fuzz
float down in the gold.
I am always walking
home and it's always
summer, the ticking instrument
of the earth, the clouds,
the inexhaustible trees.

—Jenny George

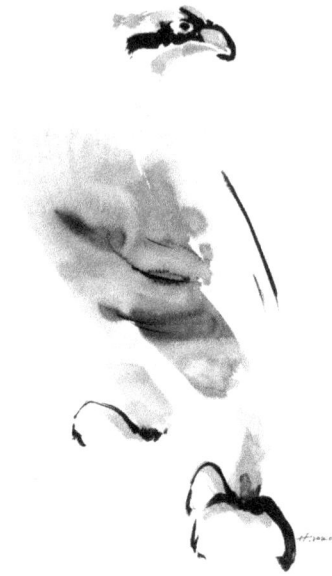

OSPREY – PANDION HALIAETUS

DESCRIPTION: The quintessential Seahawk, the Osprey is a large raptor with long, dark brown wings that have a clear bend in flight. They have a white body and head with a distinctive dark eye stripe and hooked beak. These birds dive feet first into the water to use their sharp talons to catch unsuspecting fish.

VOICE: The Osprey makes a loud, high-pitched "chirp-chirp-chirp" whistle, which they may repeat for a long time.

HABITAT: With a diet of fish, Ospreys are found near bodies of water April through September. They nest on tall structures—not only trees, but utility poles and artificial nesting platforms as well. Ospreys are monogamous and return to the same nest sites year after year. Both parents help build the nest and care for the young.

INTRIGUING TIDBIT: Ospreys are the most widespread raptor in the world. They can be found on every continent except Antarctica.

DATE AND LOCATION SEEN:

Osprey's Duet

Yes, all winter I have been down in Mazatlán,
reveling at the warm shore, eyeing the water's
depths, plunging, hooking a delectable silver fish
in each taloned claw. But still, I've thought of him,
my gold-eyed bandit, his great arched wings.
I knew I would go back, the nest already there—
a little ruined, a little wind-thrown—sticks, seaweed,
bones. Yes, it took me many weeks to climb the air,
dawn, daylight, skies on fire with strange birds' music,
sunset, night smoke, past the ones who shot at me
—the angry farmer, the fishermen. Push-tired
through hail storm, following the coastline,
the river, the mountain range, riding the thermal
updraft, the corridor. There is something I know
in the blue wavelengths—a magnet's pull, circle
calling me home. I know you want to ask
about love, that you would name it, but it is more
a summoning, a *yes* in my hollow bones. A tenderness
to all the space between us and the nestlings
in each remembered song. I cross the continent
to go back to beak his masked face. I want all of it
—him tossing me a good chum, the eggs tucked
beneath my speckled snowy breast, the heat
on my wings in the noon-day sun.

—Anya Kirshbaum

RED-TAILED HAWK – BUTEO JAMAICENSIS

DESCRIPTION: Red-tailed Hawks are one of the most common and widespread raptors in Washington State. They are large hawks with broad rounded wings and a short, wide tail. While their plumage can vary, they are mostly brown with cream, barred chests and a black "belt" across their middles. They, of course, have distinctive rusty-red tails.

VOICE: The call of the Red-tailed Hawk is a raspy, descending scream that sounds like "keeer-r-r-r."

HABITAT: Red-tailed Hawks are very adaptable and can be found in a variety of habitats including forests, open countryside, and even urban areas like the I-5 corridor through the greater Seattle area. They prefer open landscapes with isolated trees and elevated perches while scanning for small mammals like rabbits, squirrels, and birds.

INTRIGUING TIDBIT: The bold screech of the Red-tailed Hawk is often used in movies and TV to substitute for the rather wimpy cry of the Bald Eagle.

DATE AND LOCATION SEEN:

Through the Valleys

The forest's upper branches were bronzed
by a falling sun. Traveling inward,
a melancholic fog of not conceiving my blessedness
descended. Then we came upon him
perched eye-level on a dead branch,
unmoving, unperturbed, on sharp lookout.

I thought of Kierkegaard's *misrelations*,
my despair like a thick grove, angled
by a red tail hawk's immortal patience.
After long while, he scattered through maple tops,
mottled breast bared, beating rusted feathers
and let out a screech above the mountain.

I am returned to myself.

—Major Jackson

SANDHILL CRANE – ANTIGONE CANADENSIS

DESCRIPTION: Sandhill Cranes are large, tall birds standing three to four feet tall with a wingspan of six to seven feet. They have long legs, long necks, and broad wings. Their plumage is mostly gray with a distinctive red patch of skin on the forehead. Social birds, they are usually seen in flocks.

VOICE: The loud trumpeting call of the Sandhill Crane can be heard from over a mile away. They also make quieter trills, purrs, and rattles.

HABITAT: Sandhill Cranes prefer grassy freshwater wetlands, bogs, marshes, prairies, and fields. Look for them during their spring and fall migration in the shallow marshes and wetlands of the Lower Columbia River or the Conboy Lake National Wildlife Refuge.

INTRIGUING TIDBIT: The mating dance of the Sandhill Crane involves quick steps and then leaping high into the air.

DATE AND LOCATION SEEN:

Dear Sandhill Crane,

I've heard you in fields and by the river
of great gatherings—symphonies of purrs
and gurgles that sound like "r"s swimming
in your throat. Even without that trumpet call,

I've heard your wings vibrate the air, long neck—
with beak that can drill a coyote's skull—
cutting the wind. You and your mate dance, call
to each other in a synchronized, complex duet.

Of the genus Antigone, you've been here
2.5 million years, survived by gathering and
foraging together for reptiles, snails,
amphibians, sorghum and waste corn.

Walking, your head moves like a snake. But
in the sky, riding the thermals, you're an arrow.

—Susan Landgraf

SORA – PORZANA CAROLINA

DESCRIPTION: Soras are small, plump rails that resemble a chicken with long toes and stubby yellow bill. They have a blue-grey face, chest and belly, and brown mottled cap and back. They have a black face mask.

VOICE: The staccato descending call of the Sora has been described as a whinny.

HABITAT: Soras live in freshwater wetlands with dense vegetation where they can stay hidden from view. Soras skulk slowly through the vegetation, foraging on the ground for seeds and bugs that they dig up with their long toes. You are most likely to see a Sora in the early morning or late evening during their breeding season of April through July. Look in along the muddy edges of wetlands in places like the Ridgefield National Wildlife Refuge or the Skagit Wildlife Refuge.

INTRIGUING TIDBIT: Despite appearing to be weak fliers, Soras regularly migrate long distances, with many traveling to South America for the winter.

DATE AND LOCATION SEEN:

On the Boardwalk

at Billy Frank Jr. Nisqually Wildlife Refuge

Come Sora, youth of a brood, move your
little chick torso into these marshy waters.

Amid the tall grasses,
you grow, play hide 'n seek among cattails
with birders, where they listen to your whinny.

No, you are fowl, not a foal, but each whinny
and wee echoes across the wetland.

You saunter the mud, little rail
as your squat tail stirs and rakes water for seeds,
your orange beak pecks, and you swallow a snail.

How long will you stay until you soar south,
oh, small balloon of a bird, size of a football?

I wish you cartographies
of wetlands to descend, rest during migration,
until you return north, here, to weave a new nest.

—Mary Ellen Talley

TURKEY VULTURE – CATHARTES AURA

DESCRIPTION: Turkey Vultures are a large, dark-colored bird with a featherless red head and red bills with ivory colored tips. They use their impressive 5–6 foot wingspan to soar on thermals and air currents, gliding effortlessly for long periods of time. Their distinctive V-shaped, two-toned wings help to distinguish them from other large birds of prey.

VOICE: Since Turkey Vultures lack a syrinx (vocal organ), they are generally silent. If needed, they make a low hiss or grunt.

HABITAT: Turkey Vultures like a mix of open spaces for foraging, and woodlands and rocky outcroppings for communal roosting and nesting. They use a keen sense of smell to locate dead animals, their primary food source. You are most likely to see Turkey Vultures April through September while cruising open areas and highways like Highway 2 in the Wenatchee River Valley.

INTRIGUING TIDBIT: Turkey Vultures use defensive projectile vomiting to warn off predators.

DATE AND LOCATION SEEN:

Scavengers

As a fully fleshed queer I'm sure I speak for all of the community when I say that I aspire to be a Turkey Vulture.

They are, after all, the baddest bitches on the block. Don't we all tremble with envy over their impeccable aesthetic? Over their wrinkly shaved heads and bone-colored beaks? Don't we all sigh with longing when they bring fear on the merits of style alone?

For it's hardly their habits that inspire animosity. They're scavengers after all, cleaning up those sad hunks of meat that make us flinch when we encounter them on long stretches of road. The most admirable custodians of the highway.

And it can hardly be annoyance that motivates disgust. No loud squawking, no shrieking in the early morning. They lack a voice after all, some trick of evolution leaving them without a syrinx.

So, why wouldn't I wish to be a Turkey Vulture? Me, who loves my community and my queerness with an open-hearted devotion? There's a kinship here, with this voiceless scavenger.

A creature scorned with no regard for their nature.

—Mulch Morwell

SHOREBIRDS

BLACK OYSTERCATCHER – HAEMATOPUS BACHMANI

DESCRIPTION: All black with a striking long orange-red bill, red eyes, and short pink legs, the Black Oystercatcher can't be mistaken for any other bird. This is a medium-sized shorebird found year-round in Washington, but only in a few locations on Washington's coasts like Point Grenville.

VOICE: The call of a Black Oystercatcher is a loud repetitive, high-pitched "wheep, wheep, wheep."

HABITAT: In coastal areas, Black Oystercatchers forage at low tide on rocky shorelines using their strong bills to pry open mussels, limpets, and other shellfish. Despite their name, the Black Oystercatcher rarely eats oysters. Look for them in places like Whidbey Island and the San Juan Islands.

INTRIGUING TIDBIT: Black Oystercatchers gather in pairs or family groups and are very long-lived. They can have a lifespan of up to 20 years.

DATE AND LOCATION SEEN:

After Leaving, a Name

I want a life where all I do
is eat mussels. To use my body
in all its mechanical ripeness, an
orange key unlocking pearly brine:
all mine. Late August along this rocky
shore and I am walking two years after my
kind-of divorce, barnacles crushed to porcelain
dust underneath. Clams spit a bridge of water across
my salt stunned face, spigot of self. Oystercatchers don't
really eat oysters, I learn. Instead: mussels, limpets. How strange to
name something that it's not. Like me, a Wife, not. Musselcatcher,
Limpetlover, Blacknailpolishfootedforager, imagine a name
that fits your feverish flash of neon light. The language
of birds is untranslatable. But if I could allow myself
this shored song, spend each day swallowing
minor moons of tidal meat, what would
I call myself, how might I speak?

—Jane Wong

DUNLIN – CALIDRIS ALPINA

DESCRIPTION: The Dunlin is a small sandpiper with a distinctive black drooping bill and black legs. When in Washington, they are not usually seen in their breeding plumage with black-brown belly patch and rusty feathers. Their non-breeding plumage is a uniformly grayish brown with a white belly. They are very social birds found in large flocks in winter. These birds fly by the thousands in tight, choreographed groups, flashing the dark and light sides of their wings in sync.

VOICE: The Dunlin has a soft, short, and raspy "kree."

HABITAT: Fall through spring, the Dunlin can be found in estuaries, mudflats, marshes, and coastal wetlands. They feed by probing their long bills into the mud and sand, searching for worms, bugs, and crustaceans.

INTRIGUING TIDBIT: The Dunlin is the most common shorebird in Washington and is considered an indicator species for assessing the health of their ecosystem.

DATE AND LOCATION SEEN:

Dunlins

Their white breasts
turn on wind, mosaics
of fifty, more, fewer
than the year before,
trill on one wing,
zing off a wave,
then light on eelgrass
heaped in thinner cords
than last year's.
They scatter,
peck sand fleas,
far fewer now too, three
seconds, five, then
whose idea to swarm
on drafts off waves?
To whiplash till
they wipe each blue
from sky and sleep
—but where?—
to lift off, flash
in dim first light
and vanish.

—Michael Daley

GREATER YELLOWLEGS – TRINGA MELANOLEUCA

Description: The Greater Yellowlegs is a large sandpiper with long, bright yellow legs. Their wings are speckled and mottled brown in winter and black in breeding plumage. Their bellies are white. They sport long necks and long, slim, and slightly upturned bills. The high stepping gait and bob of the Greater Yellowlegs help them forage in shallow waters.

VOICE: The call of the Greater Yellowlegs is a series of three to four descending notes that sound like "tew, tew, tew."

HABITAT: Greater Yellowlegs live in freshwater and marine wetland environments like saltwater marshes, mudflats, estuaries, and shallow ponds and lakes. Look for them year-round in places like the Snoqualmie Valley wetlands or the San Juan Islands.

INTRIGUING TIDBIT: When a predator approaches, Greater Yellowlegs are some of the first shorebirds to sound an alarm. This helps to alert other birds in the area.

DATE AND LOCATION SEEN:

All About Me, the Greater Yellowlegs

My legs are as yellow as bananas, lemons, the sun,
    yellow markers, and yellow-colored pencils.
They're as long as a tightrope, a crane, a long stick,
    a playground slide, and my imagination.

My eyes are as small as marbles, as *Cheerios*, as a bouncy ball,
    and a chocolate chip.
They're as black as iron, a black dog, midnight, a crow, and
    burnt wood.

My beak is as sharp as a knife, a shark's tooth, a dinosaur's
    tooth, scissors, a spear, a tweezer,
a needle to draw blood, and a port needle.

My body is shaped like an oval, an egg.

My feathers are gray and black, and pointy, sharp.

My tail is a triangle.

Now, what about you?

—Student collaboration by five youths at Seattle Children's

KILLDEER – CHARADRIUS VOCIFERUS

DESCRIPTION: The Killdeer is a medium-sized brown and black shorebird with two distinctive black bands across their white chest, and a brown, black, and white-striped face. They have large eyes with a red eye ring and a medium bill typical to plovers.

VOICE: The loud, shrill, and repetitive "kill-dee, kill-dee, kill-deer" call has given Killdeer their odd name.

HABITAT: Although technically a shorebird, the Killdeer can be found far from water, in open areas like grasslands, agricultural fields, and golf courses, as well as shorelines of lakes and rivers eating insects, worms, and snails.

INTRIGUING TIDBIT: The Killdeer is known for faking a broken wing to lure predators away from their nests—shallow and exposed indentations in the sand.

DATE AND LOCATION SEEN:

No Deer Were Injured in the Writing of this Poem

Like the *chick-a-dee-dee-dee*, they were named
for their song—*kill-deer, kill-deer*—a high shriek
across a sapphire sky or a single song in the dark.

Ground nester. In the sand dunes, the high
grass, spring becomes a season of threats
—beachcomber with black lab, coyote,

raccoons, foxes, crows, and gulls. Dear
Chattering Plover, Dear Noisy Plover, your call
is your calling card. Your name is so misleading

—*killdeer*—so harsh, as if Bambi is ready to be
slain in the forest. Though you are not a hunter,
but a protector. Like when danger approaches

your nest, you fake a broken wing so the stray
cat follows what looks to be an injured bird
across the gravel road, across the meadow, gone

from the nest you built. And once far away
your faux-broken wing act ends. The cat begins
to pounce on your small body and like that—

you take flight! Precocial chicks safe, a cat left
perplexed, your call a bubbling trill across
the blue, laughter echoing above the shore.

—Kelli Russell Agodon

LEAST SANDPIPER – CALIDRIS MINUTILLA

DESCRIPTION: The Least Sandpiper is a small shorebird, about the size of a sparrow, with brownish upper parts, white lower parts streaked with brown on the chest. They have yellow legs and a short, thin, black bill.

VOICE: The chatty Least Sandpiper's call is described as a musical, high-pitched, trilled "preep."

HABITAT: You can find the Least Sandpiper in wetland habitats like coastal mudflats, inland wet meadows, flooded fields, and the edges of lakes, ponds, and ditches. They adopt a hunched posture when foraging for small invertebrates. Look for them during their spring or fall migration in places like Grays Harbor National Wildlife Refuge or Turnbull National Wildlife Refuge where you'll find them foraging in the upper edges of mudflats, higher up than the other sandpipers.

INTRIGUING TIDBIT: The Least Sandpiper is the smallest shorebird in the world, weighing in at only 1 ounce. Yet, they can fly non-stop for 1800–2500 miles during migration.

DATE AND LOCATION SEEN:

To Say the Least

is to say the smallest—
is to say that's no twitch of the eye.
It's like saying there exists
in the world of peeps
some greater, faster shoreline speedwalker.
To spot the leasts—
time-lapse stitchers of the strand
—to hear their pin-piped *preet*
is to count the least
among us.

—Katy E. Ellis

MARBLED GODWIT – LIMOSA FEDOA

DESCRIPTION: The Marbled Godwit is a large shorebird with a long, thin, and slightly upturned bill. They are a mottled brown with cinnamon underwings and black legs.

VOICE: The call of the Marbled Godwit is a loud and nasal "ga-wit, ga-wit," reminiscent of their name.

HABITAT: As with other shorebirds, you can find Marbled Godwits on Washington's coastal mudflats, salt marshes, and estuaries. Look for them in the winter at Tokeland in Willapa Bay or the docks of Westport where they roost and feed in large groups.

INTRIGUING TIDBIT: When foraging, the Marbled Godwit can insert their entire bill into the mud, sometimes even completely submerging their heads.

DATE AND LOCATION SEEN:

Eventually, Birds Must Land

The godwits flew south through the Pacific. They did not
stop at islands along the way. Instead, they traveled up to
7,100 miles in nine days...
        −Robert E. Gill Jr., *The New York Times*

Imagine the whole ocean   Flying it over
days   miles   Sleep   as another

name for auto-pilot

Ocean
no

land   Sleep with wings spread   water
below   five thousand miles

to the fore

Imagine
God

beyond the confines of a week

One must open   to belief
in horizon line

of above
and under

navigating wind   swells rearing
How many breaths before death
is overcome

ocean-locked
stretch

Sea and sky as a means
to breaking   open

Land
         the lover
beyond the seam

                        —Ronda Piszk Broatch

SANDERLING – CALIDRIS ALBA

DESCRIPTION: The Sanderling is a small, plump shorebird that one finds in Washington only during the winter. Like other wintering shorebirds, the Sanderling's winter coloring is rather bland—a pale gray and white with black legs and a long, straight, black bill. While its coloring is bland, its behavior is not. Sanderlings distinctively run with the waves, darting in and out of the surf to feed.

VOICE: The call of the Sanderling is a soft and high-pitched peep-like sound, notably quieter than other similar shorebirds.

HABITAT: The ocean coasts of Washington are the winter home of the migratory Sanderling, though they may be found year-round in Washington. They prefer sandy beaches, mudflats in places like Ocean Shores where they run back and forth chasing the waves. This allows them to quickly access the crustaceans, mollusks, and worms freshly exposed by each retreating wave.

INTRIGUING TIDBIT: Sanderlings belong to the "Extreme Migrants" club. They can cover huge distances during their migration, moving from their Arctic breeding grounds to as far south as South America.

DATE AND LOCATION SEEN:

Beachcombers

So the shoreline likes to play, and I am
its playmate. Look at how I flirt

with the waves foaming in. My tridactyl feet
pop the bubbles. We are everywhere.

There are other birds who chase the clouds,
who adorn the trees, who snuggle with lakes

and rake the snow. We pepper the sand
and salt the sea. We are grains that hold

the shores accountable. We like to romp
in the tidal mayhem. Look at the sandbars

pocked with our footprints. Look at how
we flaunt the flats, define their edges like the last

line of defense. Look again at all the photographs
over the years. We are always here

unassuming—proof positive
of our epic existence, our glory, our glee.

We know how to play with others, Humans.
We know how to make love to the beach.

—Sandra Yannone

SNOWY PLOVER – CHARADRIUS NIVOSUS

DESCRIPTION: Snowy Plovers are small shorebirds. They have a tan head and back and white chin, chest, and belly. They have a slim but stubby black bill and a partial neck ring.

VOICE: The call of the Snowy Plover sounds like a trilled "purrrt" and a whistled "towheet."

HABITAT: You'll find Snowy Plovers on Washington's coastal beaches, dunes, and mud flats. Though year-round residents, you are more likely to see them in the winter.

INTRIGUING TIDBIT: Snowy Plovers raise multiple broods per year. They may raise up to 3 if conditions are right. The female may leave to start a new brood with a different male after the eggs hatch. Despite their prolific brooding, Snowy Plovers are listed as Endangered in Washington.

DATE AND LOCATION SEEN:

The Hurry Bird

We called them hurry birds, the snowy plovers,
running along the sand in their congregation
never close to the water like sanderlings,
just as back and forth in their hunt,
these puffs of down or seafoam on twig legs,
onyx-eyed on the lower dunes, away
from the water's edge, their nests in shallow
cups of sand left by the wind or a child's pail,
the footprint of a human, an animal track
or just an impression made by a stir of wind.
Nests lined with pebbles and bits of shell,
grasses and debris in invisible pockets of beach.
They were here just as we remember them
when we didn't know what they were called
nor that their young sing in the egg before hatching.
So much we didn't know as they hurried before us:
nesting only on open sand and never
among the grasses meant to anchor dunes,
grasses that are everywhere now where
the nests once were, or why they feigned
a broken wing when we neared them.
We know now. We know fire weather
and sea rise as they know the shadows of owls.

—Carolyn Forché

WILSON'S SNIPE – GALLINAGO DELICATA

DESCRIPTION: The Wilson's Snipe is a plump, medium-sized sandpiper with a long straight bill and relatively short legs. They are a mottled brown and black with white bellies and white streaks on their heads.

VOICE: When flushed, the Wilson's Snipe makes a harsh "scraip, scraip" call. They also make a "winnowing" sound created by their feathers when they fly.

HABITAT: Wilson's Snipes prefer the soft muddy soil found in marshes, freshwater wetlands, and flooded agricultural fields where they can probe for insects, worms, and other invertebrates. They remain in Washington year round and you can see them in places like the Ridgefield or Willapa National Wildlife Refuges.

INTRIGUING TIDBIT: The term "sniper" originated in the late 1700s among British soldiers in India who hunted the snipe for food. Those skilled enough to successfully hunt this elusive bird were referred to as "snipers" due to the precision required to hit a small, zigzagging target in flight. This term later evolved to describe military marksmen capable of hitting distant targets accurately.

DATE AND LOCATION SEEN:

Snipe Hunt

How often have I sent myself on a snipe hunt,
chasing down one fantastical folly or another
returning empty-handed to the mocking,
scoffing of my wiser self? How else
to cope with it all, but laugh? I am lost
if not for a sense of humor and an eye
on a world oblivious to foolishness,
perhaps even finding it beautiful, the way
I find a Wilson's Snipe with its dopey eyes
and cartoon beak, to be a prime example
of how not to take any of this too seriously.

—Rena Priest

WANDERING TATTLER – TRINGA INCANA

DESCRIPTION: The Wandering Tattler is a medium-sized, stocky sandpiper with dark gray chest and a white belly. The bird boasts white eyebrow stripes, a straight, dark bill, and two short yellow legs. While feeding, they make a bobbing motion.

VOICE: Wandering Tattlers make a shrill and repetitive "pee-pee-pee-pee-pee" call in flight.

HABITAT: You'll find Wandering Tattlers in rocky coastal areas, pebbly beaches, and high mountain streams. They prefer wet rocky areas where they can forage for aquatic invertebrates like crustaceans and marine worms. You are most likely to see Wandering Tattlers during their May and August-September migration period in places like the rocky jetties at Ocean Shores or Westport.

INTRIGUING TIDBIT: Wandering Tattlers protect their nests from predators by concealing them in tundra or rocky areas far from their feeding sites. They are first to sound the alarm when predators come near, earning them the name "tattlers."

DATE AND LOCATION SEEN:

Carkeek Park in Fall

It sounds like a note passed between crushes under a
    school desk—
a wandering tattler rustling rain off his feathers.

He's an anxious bird with white eyeliner and a wedge of
    brown warpaint
on his beak; a face made-up for hunting small crustaceans.

When he's still, his backside bounces like he's had
one too many cups of coffee. When he's cruising,

he scours crevices for crabs with an intensity that makes
    me wonder
if he's dropped a contact lens.

He runs up and down with the waves never allowing his feet to
    get wet;
seems appalled at the notion of being known as a "wading bird."

Along the Pacific, his *ulili* carries weight; everyone lifts their
    beaks—

—Nathan Yockey

JAEGER
—
ALCIDS
—
GULLS & TERNS

CASPIAN TERN – HYDROPROGNE CASPIA

DESCRIPTION: Caspian Terns are large, gull-like birds. Mostly white with gray wings and black legs, they have black caps that extend past their eyes and a thick bright orange-red bill.

VOICE: The call of the Caspian Tern sounds like cackling laughter.

HABITAT: You'll find Caspian Terns in aquatic environments like coastal areas, marshes, and wetlands, and large lakes and rivers. You may see them hover above the water before diving for the fish of all kinds that make up their diet. Look for their large breeding colonies at Grays Harbor or on East Sand Island on the lower Columbia River from May through August.

INTRIGUING TIDBIT: The Caspian Tern is the largest tern species in the world and is also one of the most widespread, occurring on every continent except Antarctica.

DATE AND LOCATION SEEN:

you knew this about people & birds

"They aren't laughing," she says as she turns from the riverbank into the future, towards distant street signs and dinner plans and energy bills and some faraway ocean. I remain a little longer, looking out at the estuary and the caspian terns soaring from one side of the banks to the other, their imprints barely breaking the surface of the dirt and rocks and other shadows. "They're just birds," she says as she walks away. "That's just the way they sound."

But in my mind, as they dart and glide beneath the hazy clouded morning, they are laughing at the new day together. A few fly away, tired of the joke, and others stand waiting for the rest of us, every other living creature, to understand how hilarious all of this is. These birds begin calling before they hatch—laughing at our expectations and apologies while still in the shell, all before they take their first breath of the open air we need.

Maybe their song sounds more like a scrapping than laughter, a peeling away not melodic but necessary as the grey sky lightens from the hidden sun. Maybe their call is really a blessing attempting to expose the better in everything we see. I consider this as I move away from the shores myself and look at my wife, her shoulders determined and far away now, walking towards where I should be—in a car parked just beyond our vision waiting to take us into the rising grinning imminent, what lies beyond. I try to catch up to her at the horizon striped by tall trees, all the while wondering if the clouds will ever part to reveal sunshine, and hoping that, in that spotlight, the caspian terns can tell me the punch line before I disappear.

—Stacy D. Flood

GLAUCOUS-WINGED GULL – LARUS GLAUCESCENT

DESCRIPTION: The quintessential "seagull" in the western part of the state, the large Glaucous-winged Gull is white with light gray wings and back. They have a yellow bill with a red spot at the end and pink legs and feet.

VOICE: The familiar high-pitched wail of the Glaucous-winged Gull can be heard drifting hauntingly on the air.

HABITAT: You can commonly find Glaucous-winged Gulls year-round in coastal areas, freshwater lakes, and even garbage dumps. They are highly adaptable, omnivorous, foragers who utilize various techniques including dropping shellfish onto hard surfaces to crack them open and outright stealing food from other birds.

INTRIGUING TIDBIT: Glaucous-winged Gulls can live for over 20 years.

DATE AND LOCATION SEEN:

Glaucous-Winged Attraction

People read "glaucous" like vision loss
but these gulls see fine. New companions

commune in a colony near the mouth of Hood Canal;
here, young mottled-downs molt to feathers white

then oystering to silver. She warms her wings,
sunlit, posed on a necklace of black floats,

spies him snatch greenlings from the slipstream,
dancing near a dragon made of driftwood.

His foreplay, a choke dance reveal, serves
ceviché of Dogwinkle, Storm Petrel, Sandlance.

He knows how omnivorous she can be.
Her light-winged mate never strays far,

tidefast for two seasons, his opalescence still thrills—
a sea god she'll never shun.

—Laura Urban Perry

PIGEON GUILLEMOT – CEPPHUS COLUMBA

DESCRIPTION: Pigeon Guillemots are medium-sized alcids, black with white wing patches during the breeding season. They stand out with their bold red feet and mouth lining.

VOICE: The call of the Pigeon Guillemot is described as a rapidly repeating, shrill whistle.

HABITAT: Pigeon Guillemots prefer coastal areas near rocky cliffs like those in the San Juan Islands or protected coves and bays like the Tacoma Narrows or Olympia's Budd Inlet.

INTRIGUING TIDBIT: To pursue their prey, the Pigeon Guillemot can dive up to 150 feet, using both wings and feet as propulsion.

DATE AND LOCATION SEEN:

Guillemot: Will, Desire, and Strength

Out on the bobbing waves of the Strait,
a pigeon guillemot has caught
a shiny silver fish. He shakes and shakes
it, and in a burst of joy, splashes his wings
on the water. Then, he skims, barely
above the surface, until
he's lost in shadow, toward the island shore.

Maybe there's a nest, a mate, hungry
open mouths awaiting just such a gift.

It's like joy, how hard it is sometimes
to catch it up, tiny nourishing thing,
carry it with us someplace we can share.

—Subhaga Crystal Bacon

RHINOCEROS AUKLET – CERORHINCA MONOCERATA

DESCRIPTION: The Rhinoceros Auklet is a stout, medium-sized seabird that gets their name from a white "horn" that extends from the base of their orange bill. They have a gray chest and belly with black back and wings.

VOICE: Though generally silent at sea, near the breeding grounds the calls of the Rhinoceros Auklet can be a noisy mooing, growling, braying or groaning. They are heard at night when they tend to feed their young.

HABITAT: This seabird is generally found on offshore islands and coastal areas. You will more easily see them during their spring to summer breeding season in places like Westport or the Protection Island National Wildlife Refuge.

INTRIGUING TIDBIT: The horn of the Rhinoceros Auklet is fluorescent under ultraviolet light and is thought to be used for reproductive signaling.

DATE AND LOCATION SEEN:

Glint

Grey day. Black pen. Dull air. One of those, you know?
Flaky shins, eye grit, heart a plod. I look down. Bit
of sparkle on my toenails from when my niece and I
painted in July alongside waters linked to you, bird
we might see but didn't that time and rarely
do from shore (her: not yet, me: too few), cousin
to another who wafts limequat, which doesn't matter
to this poem but I've wanted to put it in a poem for years
because a bird that smells like citrus? It's like how glitter
polish doesn't matter but it does. It does! My toes
sparkle despite me. And you, rhino, you have your own
wholly unnecessary essential, that spur toothing up
from your bill's base which hooked me, sure, lured
me to ask why and why and then in seeking find you
diving deep, wing-stroking down, and so it's not
your decoration but what you make that thrills me. Under
a ball of herring, let silver beads of air rise from your orange
gape to create a soft, open fist of light around the fish that then
you'll grab and swallow or grab and hold to bring back
to burrow. You'll satisfy yourself with a trick of whales,
little bird. By work and shine, by glimmering the dark water.

—Elizabeth Bradfield

TUFTED PUFFIN – FRATERCULA CIRRHATA

DESCRIPTION: The Tufted Puffin is a large, stocky seabird with glossy black feathers, a white face and thick red-orange bill. The red-orange extends to their legs, feet, and eye ring. They have long, golden tufts that curl over the back of their head and neck during breeding season.

VOICE: Though mostly silent, Tufted Puffins have a low growling call that sounds like "errrr."

HABITAT: You'll find Tufted Puffins in coastal areas and islands off the Washington Coast. Look for them in the summer along the Olympic Peninsula's coastal areas or Protection and Smith Islands.

INTRIGUING TIDBIT: Tufted Puffins are excellent divers and use their wings to "fly" underwater to depths of nearly 200 feet to catch small fish, like herring and squid. They also use their wings for powerful flight in the air, achieving speeds of up to 40 miles per hour.

DATE AND LOCATION SEEN:

Puff

Protection Island National Wildlife Refuge provides some
of the last remaining undeveloped habitat for many
burrow-nesting seabirds in the Salish Sea.
                          —U.S. Fish and Wildlife Service

From my desk, I see your island home nestled
in Discovery Bay. I look for signs of you

burrowing there onshore. Bonded pair
faithfully tending your single seasonal egg.

This island, your perfect habitat: rocky
bluffs and wild grasses inaccessible

to humans, secure spots for nest building.
You. Survivor of fire, storms, warming seas,

oil spills, bycatch, predation. O sister,
O brother, I lament the dwindling

numbers of your clan, mourn knowing
you were once here in abundance.

Salish winds toss me helpless against
my own thoughts, here at my desk

where I foresee your struggle to subsist.
My own footprint heavy and unsettling.

                          —Risa Denenberg

OWLS
—
PIGEONS & DOVES
—
NIGHTHAWK
—
SWIFTS

BARRED OWL – STRIX VARIA

DESCRIPTION: The Barred Owl is a medium-sized raptor with a mottled brown and white plumage appearing as brown vertical "bars" across the chest and belly that provide excellent camouflage in their forest homes. They have large dark brown eyes, a round face, and yellow bill. While primarily nocturnal, you can sometimes see the Barred Owl hunting during the day.

VOICE: The call of the Barred Owl is often described as "Who cooks for you? Who cooks for you-all?" They tend to be more vocal during the breeding season.

HABITAT: New to Washington in the mid-1960s, you can now find the invasive Barred Owls year-round near water sources such as swamps, rivers, and lakes in Washington's mature forests and other wooded regions. There, they silently hunt for small mammals, birds, amphibians, and even fish.

INTRIGUING TIDBIT: Barred Owls have specially constructed feathers with soft fringed edges that allow for nearly silent flight. This, together with their excellent low-light vision, allows them to sneak up on prey in dense forests.

DATE AND LOCATION SEEN:

What Do You Wake To?

A promise not yet broken, half a dream
where your mother is still young?

A teen's exuberant woo-HOO,
up later than late in youth and glory?

Too precise. On refrain, the round voice flew
over city rooms thick with sleeping.

When I asked the birders, I heard *Bard Owl*—
a poet raptor's last lines before dawn—

until I matched patterns of language
with the patterns of feathers.

Trees planted led one owl here.
Trees cut threaten another.

Now a plan to shoot the Barred, reserve
old growth forest for the Spotted.

As night's edges unravel, listen
again for what might call you.

—Joannie Stangeland

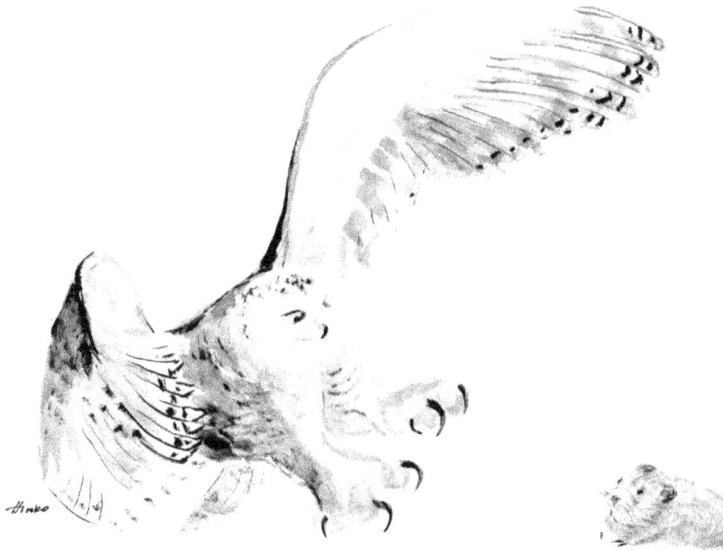

SNOWY OWL – BUBO SCANDIACUS

DESCRIPTION: The Snowy Owl is a large white owl with dark markings and large yellow eyes. Their wingspan can extend to 5 feet and they stand 2 feet tall.

VOICE: During the winter months that the Snowy Owl is in Washington, they are rarely heard.

HABITAT: Typically, Snowy Owls inhabit open tundra areas, but during times of irruption, you can find them in coastal areas, agricultural fields, and other open areas where they can hunt for small mammals and other prey. Diurnal hunters, the Snowy Owl is one of the few owls that are active during the day. In the winter months of an irruption year, look for Snowy Owls in places like Damon Point in Ocean Shores.

INTRIGUING TIDBIT: Irruptions are sudden and irregular movements of a large number of owls moving much farther south than usual, perhaps as far as Florida. Irruptions can happen every four to five years, driven by an abundance of prey during the breeding season leading to large broods and a need for young owls to disperse.

DATE AND LOCATION SEEN:

Here's Marveling at You, from the Gray Gabled Roof on Seattle's Queen Anne Hill

while you marvel at me, a Snowy Owl from the Arctic tundra, wet with fog. I should be up at the Canadian border. Or at Damon Point at Ocean Shores. At least that's what they say.

I say, owl feathers! It's fate to marvel at you while you marvel at me—the great Bubo scandiacus, of the order Strigiformes, of the family Strigidae; of the tubular eyes, yellow, like a blaze of yarrow. Bubo scandiacus, of the asymmetrical ears to hear all that skitters, even beneath snow. A nomad, mostly solo, except when I fall in love.

Here's to you, nine-year-old marvel in your dancing feet, your smile as wide as my five-foot wingspan, your indigo jacket puffed with duck feathers—that's okay. With binoculars on your face, you cheer, "Hooray!" one arm that shoots through the cloud cover. I whistle and swivel my head for you. I will call you My Marvelous Friend.

—Ann Teplick

SPOTTED OWL – STRIX OCCIDENTALIS CAURINA

DESCRIPTION: The Northern Spotted Owl is a medium-sized owl with brown feathers and cream streaks on the chest and belly. Their facial discs are brown with light markings between their dark brown eyes and yellowish bill.

VOICE: You'll hear a Northern Spotted Owl make a deep four-note call sounding like "hoo-hoo-hoo-hooooo."

HABITAT: The Northern Spotted Owl came into popular awareness because of its very particular habitat needs—old growth coniferous forests in low to mid elevation areas. They need large trees for nesting and dense canopy cover for roosting and foraging. An indicator species, their presence signals a mature, healthy forest ecosystem. While you might find Northern Spotted Owls in Washington year-round, loss of habitat and competition with the more adaptable and invasive Barred Owl makes sightings increasingly rare.

INTRIGUING TIDBIT: Logging of old growth forests dramatically reduced the habitat of the Northern Spotted Owl. As a result, they are protected by the Endangered Species Act. which prohibits them from being harassed or disturbed.

DATE AND LOCATION SEEN:

It Was the Best Two-Year Job

It was like I had a personal connection,

with the spotted owls. You hoot back and forth, feed them
(lab mice on a limb), make up names, glitz them with a leg
band, get strafed by talons, measure them. I also found myself
in remote ancient forests few people had stepped in before.
Massive spruce, fir and maple trees stood so tall, some toppled
like tidily-winks, with thick moss draped over everything like
curtains or hoods.

The thrill of hearing their call meant you might lure them
with your own hoots. The discovery of all these mating pairs in
Olympic National Park was incredible, but it just so happened,
concurrently, barred owls started invading their territory,
hunting them down, running them out of their dwindling
home turf—they're slower to adapt these relics of hoot-dom.

It is rarer now to hear the spotted owl's four beat bark, but
they're still found, their forlorn calls echo amongst the
changing landscape. It took a long time before I found a job
nearly as satisfying, but I ultimately became a teacher, which
is oddly similar—at how I tend to my student's needs, with
their wild yelps seeking connection and attention, procreation
forefront in their minds, me getting strafed, helplessly
watching them from afar, with dangerous interlopers

everywhere.

—Lowell Jons

CHUKAR PARTRIDGE – ALECTORIS CHUKAR

DESCRIPTION: Chukar Partridges are plump game birds with a distinctive black band that extends from the forehead, through the eyes, and down the neck. They have tan bodies with black streaks and red legs and bills.

VOICE: The call of a Chukar Partridge sounds like their name "chuk-chuck-chuck-ar."

HABITAT: Steep rocky areas with sagebrush and grasslands are comfortable places for the Chukar Partridge. Look for them in the breaks of the Columbia River north of Wenatchee.

INTRIGUING TIDBIT: Chukars were brought to the US from Eurasia for hunting. They are great runners and can navigate steep, rocky slopes with ease.

DATE AND LOCATION SEEN:

Red Legs

For the beautiful partridge of the pheasant family
called Chukar

We saw you in India, dipping down to the tank, as everyone
    called it,
right before the sun sank. You walked cheerfully toward the
    water,
oblivious to bigger birds, your red legs confident on sand.
Chukar, how have you come so far? Oman to Palestine, Dead Sea,
even Hawai'i, your tail has only 14 feathers. What could you
    teach
the crazy humans about coexistence, *chuck chuck chukar*
    chukar your
chant of peace, maybe your heart has 144 hopes. We need your
    wisdom
drenching us in our desert. I'm lonely for everything I believed
as a child. We can be friends with anyone. Wars are dumb. Even
    though
you are hunted in Washington and Oregon, our own civilized
    gun-loving land,
you still make a stand there. I read some very crucial notes
about you. You are "relatively unaffected by loss of habitat."
Bless the Gazans please, expected to conduct their days in a
    heap of rubble.
"When disturbed you prefer to run rather than fly." Bless their
    own thin legs.
Make the ground their sky.

—Naomi Shihab Nye

COMMON NIGHTHAWK – CHORDEILES MINOR

DESCRIPTION: Common Nighthawks are medium-sized birds, slightly larger than an American Robin. Their dark plumage is a mix of gray, black, brown, and white that makes for excellent camouflage when they are resting in trees or on the ground. They are often seen in flight, where you can observe their long slender wings with distinctive white bars at wingtips, tails, and chin. They have small beaks and large mouths.

VOICE: In flight, the Common Nighthawk makes a repetitive nasal "beent" call.

HABITAT: You can find Common Nighthawks in Eastern Washington's open areas: grasslands, forest clearings, gravelly riverbeds, and even urban areas. They are active during the dawn and dusk twilight, catching insects. Look for them late May through August in places like the Palouse region or the Columbia River Gorge.

INTRIGUING TIDBIT: Despite their name, Common Nighthawks are neither strictly nocturnal nor are they related to hawks. They belong to a group of birds called nightjars and are more closely related to swifts and hummingbirds.

DATE AND LOCATION SEEN:

Duskeater

Insectivore! No hook-beaked bird of prey
He waits to play on skyline silhouettes
When midges rise to swell the placid air
A fly-specked feast suspended in his path

Deployed across the skyline silhouettes
His white-patched elbows flashing with each flap
A fly-specked banquet yielding to his path
Then hoovered down the cavern of his throat

His white-patched elbows flashing with each flap
A raucous *beeent* electrifies the gloom
Resounding from the cavern of his throat
He boomerangs to reel another catch

His raucous *beeent* electrifies the gloom
His acrobatic hunger flays the sky
A boomerang that you could never catch
Misnamed, voracious, cheerful in his cry

—Robbie Gamble

MOURNING DOVE – ZENAIDA MACROURA

DESCRIPTION: Mourning Doves are slender, medium-sized birds with light gray and brown plumage. They have round heads and brown eyes, with blue eye rings. They have black spots on their wings and a long, tapered tail bordered in white.

VOICE: You may have heard the "coo-ah, coo-coo-coo" of the Mourning Dove and mistaken it for an owl. The mournful sound is also the source of their name. Mourning Doves also make a whistling sound which is produced by their wings during takeoff and landing.

HABITAT: Mourning Doves can be found in a variety of open environments including farms, parks, woodlands, and forest edges. They are also comfortable in suburban settings. They dwell year-round throughout Washington but are more plentiful in Eastern Washington where they enjoy semi-open areas like that found in the Columbia Basin.

INTRIGUING TIDBIT: Most birds have one or two broods per year. The Mourning Dove, however, can have up to six broods a year. Both parents care for the young; generally keeping long-term monogamous bonds.

DATE AND LOCATION SEEEN:

Hunted

oh, how you grieve her, dear bird,
the rain dove who loved you and died,
shot while rising into the bright ring of day,
the sound held in the dark of your sad eye
as your wings whistle the air,
clear of the hunter with you, too, in his sights,

mourning dove, dove mourning

clear of the hunter with you, too, in his sights,
as your wings whistle the air,
the sound held in the dark of your sad eye,
shot while rising into the bright ring of day,
the rain dove who loved you and died,
dear bird, oh, how you grieve her.

—Geraldine Mills

ROCK PIGEON – COLUMBA LIVIA

DESCRIPTION: Rock Pigeons are medium-sized, compact birds with a stout body, round head, and short neck. Their bill is short and slender. They have broad pointed wings and a wide tail. Unlike most other birds, Rock Pigeons vary in coloration and one bird can look very different from the next. This variety is the result of being bred by humans.

VOICE: The soft "coo-coo-coo" of the Rock Pigeon is a familiar sound in cityscapes and is just one of the many vocalizations that Rock Pigeons have.

HABITAT: Rock Pigeons are highly adaptable and can be found in urban areas near buildings and bridges or in rural settings like farmland, parks, and gardens. Their original habitat was coastal rocky cliffs or ledges like those in the Columbia River Gorge. You can find them year-round in Washington in any city square.

INTRIGUING TIDBIT: Rock Pigeons have remarkable homing abilities, using magnetoreception and sun-compass orientation for navigation. The famous homing pigeons are a domesticated version of the Rock Pigeon.

DATE AND LOCATION SEEN:

The Common Pigeon: An Assay

Called Rock Dove, *Columba livia,*
Palomia brava, "rats with wings"—
of all birds, surely the most ignored,
dishonored, despised.
No birder exults, adding you to their life list.

On the dinner plate: squab.

And yet:
Able to fly 93 miles per hour on your black-barred wings.

Your longest recorded flight: 7200 miles,
France to Saigon, in twenty-four days.

One 1918 trench-taken messenger pigeon,
Kaiser, holds your record life-span: thirty-one years.
Also, America's longest-held POW.
First victory-paraded, then kept for breeding.

Another messenger,
shot down and battle-blinded on the Meuse-Argonne line,
took wing again, delivered the capsuled note:
*"We are along the road parallel to 276.4. Our own artillery is
dropping a barrage directly on us. For heaven's sake, stop it."*
One hundred and ninety-four soldiers lived.

As did Cher Ami, saved by an Army medic,
given the French *Croix de Guerre.*
Now standing in a Smithsonian display case, on one
        taxidermied leg.

Domesticable, a consorter with humans.
For this, your lives are treated, too often, as ours are.

Subject of many studies and books. For instance,
Making Pigeons Pay: A Manual of Practical Information on

the Management, Selection, Breeding, Feeding, and Marketing of
    Pigeons,
© 1946 by Wendell Mitchell Levi. Once a child who raised pigeons.

Some who keep you in rooftop pens and train you to race
have loved you,
waiting for months for one who didn't return.

City-falcons hunt you.
City-humans, sitting on benches, share with you their lonely bread.

Your ring-necked cousins
arrive each late June to eat my tree's ripening mulberries.
Crows larger, louder, less peaceful, come then to drive them away.

Your average weight, a large coffee mug's twelve ounces.
Your lives in the wild, 2.4 years.
Wing tip to wing tip, you stretch roughly twenty-three inches.

Your first-light conversations
held on an air conditioner's twelfth-story pigeon-sized ledge—
even the furious-at-being-wakened recognize this sound as true
affection.

We, who tell children they must not touch you,
gave you this habitat and story.

You are like us. You want to live.
You do what you must. You preen. You scavenge.
Are kept—like us—off a place you might rest on
only by spools of barbed wire. Are shooed. Are cursed.

Like ours, your newborn are helpless.

You live amidst and between us concealing your nests,
your dead, the first awkward flights
of your young.
You share the tending of eggs, the feeding of hatchlings.

Like us, you have learned the timing of stoplights.
Like us, you are adaptable, resilient, ingenious.
You return, when it is needed, to dwelling on cliffs.

Meaning: you will be among the slower to vanish.
Meaning also: among the longer to suffer.

You will glean, like us,
this world for as long as you can.
Lift with your strong, slightly comical cere-topped beaks
its joy-scraps, grief-crusts, recalcitrant seeds.

In flocks crowding any corner and park,
you hide amid flapping flusters and flushes of iridescence
your pigeonish judgments, jokes, meditations,

keeping also opaque from our knowing the instruments—
magnetic? aural? optic-nerve sextant?—
of your solitary, almost spiritual, home-seeking navigation.

—Jane Hirshfield

VAUX'S SWIFT – CHAETURA VAUXI

DESCRIPTION: Swifts come by their names honestly, as one of the fastest flying birds, reaching speeds of over 100 mph. The Swift's torpedo-shaped body is blackish-brown, and they flap their wings rapidly in flight, rarely gliding.

VOICE: The Swift has a rapid, high-pitched twittering call.

HABITAT: Swifts are summer residents in Washington. They are almost always in the air, flying over forests and wetlands seeking small insects to eat while flying (also known as "on the wing"). They nest and roost communally in hollow trees or in urban areas, smokestacks, and chimneys in places like Olympia or Yakima.

INTRIGUING TIDBIT: The Swift has very tiny feet and short legs making it difficult to walk or perch.

DATE AND LOCATION SEEN:

The Swifts

One August night, ten thousand.
Four thousand now, in this long, September dusk.
Some repeaters, staying over.

No first growth stumps in sight–
no forests at all on this stretch of flyway—
and so they roost in a school's brick chimney,
ten thousand then, four thousand now,

turning in wide, counterclockwise gyres
above the chimney's rusted clockface, turning
their four-inch, half-ounce shapes, three heartbeats
per wingbeat, three heartbeats per clipped syllable
of each high-pitched cry, some repeaters,

staying over. Just to the west,
the sunset that stains their bellies
to the dusky gold of mine canaries

slips over the gray Pacific, while to the east, under
Kentucky and Illinois, the root-tips of fossil forests
reach down through the roofs of coalmine shafts.
Tropical then, the trees, three hundred million years ago,

rain-filled, before the planet quickly warmed
and the magma shifted and the world's first birds
cast their neuronic blips
and the world's first flocks answered in unison.
What? the miner's asked, brushed on the nape

by a weightlessness three hundred million years
whittled. Only the roots of absence, tepid
across the skin. And tangible in that darkness

as the sudden blip that any moment now
will draw this flock, like airborne ash, backward

through the chimney. The cell-phone camera eyes,
like miners' headlamps, tip up in unison

toward a micro-ounce of source too swift
for mystery. Wing dip? Cell click? Could the answer
be corporeal? Attention to the matter?
Their eyes are bigger than their beaks. Their sleep
no opposable toes—is vertical. Just to the west,

A line of contrails draws us—
and down they drop, wings tucked, past
the chipped mortar and carbon dust, past the open flue,
the first birds overlapped by the next, and those

by the next, and next, climbing the chimney's shadow shape
in four-inch repetitions. Ten thousand then,
four thousand now, upright on the bricks.

—Linda Bierds

Hiroko

WESTERN SCREECH OWL – MEGASCOPS KENNICOTTII

DESCRIPTION: The Western Screech Owl is a small, stocky owl with a round head, yellow eyes, and ear tufts. They are usually brown or gray with mottled markings on their chests that help them blend in with the trees.

VOICE: The call of the Western Screech Owl is a series of soft hoots that accelerate in the manner of a dropping ping pong ball.

HABITAT: You can find Western Screech Owls year-round in a variety of wooded habitats, particularly those with cottonwood, aspen, and oak trees. Their varied diet ranges from insects to fish to birds, making them highly adaptable to even urban environments. Look for them in spring in large wooded parks like Lincoln Park in Seattle.

INTRIGUING TIDBIT: Despite the name, Western Screech Owls don't actually screech.

DATE AND LOCATION SEEN:

Screech Owl

All night each reedy whinny
from a bird no bigger than a heart
flies out of a tall black pine
and, in a breath, is taken away
by the stars. Yet, with small hope
from the center of darkness
it calls out again and again.

—Ted Kooser

HUMMINGBIRDS
—
KINGFISHER
—
WOODPECKERS
—
FALCONS
—
FLYCATCHERS

AMERICAN KESTREL – FALCO SPARVERIUS

DESCRIPTION: The American Kestrel is North America's smallest falcon, about the same size as an American Robin. They are also remarkably colorful for a raptor with a blue-gray head and wings, rusty-red back, a spotted chest, and a bold black marking on either side of their face—resembling a drooping mustache. They also have black eye spots on the back of their heads to deter predators from approaching from behind.

VOICE: A high pitched and repetitive "kilee-kilee-kilee-kilee" alerts one to the presence of an American Kestrel, often before spotting the bird itself.

HABITAT: Though highly adaptable, the American Kestrel prefers open habitats like grasslands and agricultural areas with scattered trees, utility wires, or other high perches. They can use high perches or hoover above open ground to search for small mammals, birds, even insects—catching their prey by diving swiftly from above.

INTRIGUING TIDBIT: The American Kestrel can see ultraviolet (UV) light. This allows kestrels to track mice and other prey by their urine trails, which reflect ultraviolet light.

DATE AND LOCATION SEEN:

little spell for kestrel hovering / for x-ray & mothering

if you watch in slow motion / the flecked kestrel / on Youtube
/ you'll watch your own lungs fanning out against the sun /
sweet girl made of March light through a seed pod / how delta
the vein & heart / highways of breath, of atmospheric capacity
/ fluctuating twenty times a minute / like fleck on fleck on
feather / remember smiling? / remember your joy wrinkles? /
you could fix your eyes on this bird / as if it holds a wavelength
in the electromagnetic spectrum / while it stays in one place /
above the rocky cliffs / while it hunts / barely wind-ruffled, on
the heather / while it lands, feasting with that beautiful beak
/ literally eating the small snake alive / below this spectacle
so many colorful tents / on the beaches / people picnicking on
dead meat / & building castles / & dressing & undressing their
wingless offspring / those lumpy but language-gifted gods

—Maya Jewell Zeller

ANNA'S HUMMINGBIRD – CALYPTE ANNA

DESCRIPTION: Anna's Hummingbirds are remarkable birds in many respects. Their tiny bodies maintain wings that beat up to 80 times per second, allowing the hummingbird to fly backwards, the only bird that can do so.

VOICE: This diminutive bird has a distinctive, high-pitched buzzy chirp.

HABITAT: Although not found in Washington before the 1960s, the Anna's hummingbird now lives year-round in parks and residential areas, dining on nectar and insects. Their range continues to grow, encouraged by winter feeders and climate change. Fairly common in Western Washington, you can also commonly find Anna's Hummingbirds in places like Wenatchee and Yakima.

INTRIGUING TIDBIT: The Anna's Hummingbird was named after Anna Masséna, the Duchess of Rivoli, who lived in the 1800s.

DATE AND LOCATION SEEN:

Renaming Anna's Hummingbird

Call me Scarlett Bottle Rocket, Love Nectars, Helicopter
of the Heliotrope, Queen of the Spider Webs
Wintering. Call me Hot Lips Sugar-Blossom, Candy Crooner,
call me Watermelon-Kisser. I think you might be a flower
in your red dress, I think you might plant the tallest
penstemon. I am sipping the purple lupins, deep diving
in the bee balm, I have come for the sweetness, to winter
near the soft cup I have woven in the junipers. I have
tucked it in the branches there, a womb of one inch
for the tiny white jelly beans, my two darlings. I know
you think I am your grandmother, I know you want to stroke
the impossible iridescence at my throat, that you wish
to pin me to your poem. But I'm just zipping through—
a little myth troubling the air, so fast a green blur,
a question you can't answer. Call me Toothless
Cartographer, Tiny Astral Bloom, Firework in Full Daylight.
I am just upside down here, split tonguing the red
columbine. A little zigzag of tiny gods. I know
that you love me a little. But I have caught a good updraft,
winged so fast you can't see. A talisman tucked in
to the cascara tree. Call me Scarlet Sun Drop, Fierce
Little Vector, call me Treble Clef. I know you have hung
a saucer of sweet-water from your eaves. But I'm out liquoring
in the sugar sages, gathering the aphids, the microscopic
midges. I think you ought to join—sink your tongue
into the coral honeysuckle, you strange un-feathered
animal, you funny two-legged thing—slow and hunched, a bit
lost. Call me Wind Tumbler, Winged Wheelbarrow, Shooting
Star of the Funneling Fuchsia. I'm knitting the spider's silk,
the lichens, pushing in the thistle down. A little lightning flash,
priestess of the gooseberries, dive bombing the morning.

—Anya Kirshbaum

CALLIOPE HUMMINGBIRD – SELASPHORUS CALLIOPE

DESCRIPTION: The smallest breeding bird in North America, the Calliope Hummingbird is small even for a hummingbird, measuring only 3 inches and weighing only 2.5 grams. They have a very short tail and relatively short bill. They possess an iridescent green head, back, and tail. Their chests and bellies are a buff-gray with a streaked magenta throat.

VOICE: The name, "Calliope," means "beautiful voiced." However, this hummingbird is fairly quiet with quiet "chip" sounds while foraging and a sharp "zing" sound during dives.

HABITAT: Ponderosa pines, Grand Firs, and Douglas Firs are favorite habitats of the Calliope Hummingbird. You may also see them at your hummingbird feeder. Look for them late April through early September in open forests and brushy areas primarily east of the Cascades, including places like the Blue Mountains.

INTRIGUING TIDBIT: Calliope Hummingbirds are named after Calliope, the Greek muse of poetry and eloquence.

DATE AND LOCATION SEEN:

Calliope

Just a few grams of glitter and hover.
If you were a dream
no one would believe in you,
the sparkling wine of your gorget, your stiletto bill.
You've been called a feathered jewel,
a hue of roses steeped in liquid fire.
You're a spill of iridescence,
a hundred thousand splintered mirrors reflecting the sun.
Aerial acrobat, packet
of embers ascending. Crushed light.
One forkful of the luster universe,
and fierce, fast, you can claw and stab.
You aim, when you need to,
straight for the eye.

—Ellen Bass

BELTED KINGFISHER – MEGACERYLE ALCYON

DESCRIPTION: A medium-sized bird with a large head and shaggy crest, the Belted Kingfisher looks dressed for an evening out with a distinctive slate blue head, back, and wings, and white underbelly. Belted Kingfishers are known for their amazing fishing skills. They sit on a perch or hover over water to locate the prey, then they dive, headfirst, into the water to catch the fish with their sharp beaks.

VOICE: The Belted Kingfisher has a loud, high-pitched rattling call that sounds like a series of rapid "kek-kek-kek" notes.

HABITAT: Seen year-round near still water with good sightlines like Seattle's Union Bay Natural Area, the Belted Kingfisher eats small fish that it pounds to death before swallowing headfirst. They seek out sandy banks for nesting—digging nesting burrows of up to 6 feet long.

INTRIGUING TIDBIT: The Belted Kingfisher has excellent vision and can see underwater. They also have special bones in their skulls to protect them from brain damage resulting from the high impact of their fishing techniques.

DATE AND LOCATION SEEN:

To the Kingfisher

My quiet tear, my small
marvel, my wingwisher,

I try to keep sorrow
away from your nest,
but you settle. You settle

then fly to the telephone wire
where the pulse of sadness
moves beneath your feet

—do not listen.

It is the human world calling
and they are always crying.

—Kelli Russell Agodon

MERLIN – FALCO COLUMBARIUS

DESCRIPTION: Merlins are small, compact falcons with pointed wings visible while flying. They have blue-grey head and wings and dark streaking on their chests, deeply banded tails, and yellow legs.

VOICE: The rapid, high-pitched call of the Merlin is described as "kee-kee-kee."

HABITAT: Merlins prefer relatively open landscapes like grasslands, parks, forest edges, and even urban areas. They live in Washington year-round, but you are more likely to see them during spring and fall migrations. Look in places like Eastern Washington prairies or coastal areas like Ocean Shores.

INTRIGUING TIDBIT: You might find a mated pair of Merlins engaging in cooperative hunting—working together using remarkable speed and surprise to flush out and capture their prey, like songbirds.

DATE AND LOCATION SEEN:

A Nest Becomes a Nest

Alakazam.

Twi, Twi—

From the tip of an old hemlock in a trailhead parking lot, small, dark birdshapes dart, twitwitwi-ing, vectors direct, powerful. Some seasons ago crows found the hemlock and assembled a twig nest bolstered by sock fuzz, doll hair, and other lot leavebehinds, but as happens, abandoned it to mists and winter, and so after a thaw this season's mating merlin pairs came to hatch, fledge, and send off a new generation. A thousand years ago they were called lady hawks and noblewomen used them for hunting larks. A hundred years ago they were called pigeon hawks because that's what they look like. Alakazam. A nest becomes a nest: repurposing. A hawk becomes a hawk becomes a falcon: magic.

Also: misperception. But actually: re-perception.

They charge rather than soar, from tree to tree, hemlock to cedar to hemlock, teasing one another, issuing taunts and challenges, motivation (some of them) to nervous fledglings in their twenty-ninth day, hesitating on the precipice of first flight. Perched on the lip of their high up first home, they hop momentarily, steeling themselves for the leap. Then,

Twi, Twi, Twi, Twi, Twi, Twi, Twi

—Greg November

MYSTĒRIUM RARA AVIS

DESCRIPTION: The Mystērium Rara Avis is a small songbird distantly related to the flycatcher. The plumage is a pale purple with deep blue-gray wings and mask. They have a white eye ring and fuchsia crown, which they erect when frightened or challenged.

VOICE: Mostly silent, when they do sing, the song of the Mystērium Rara Avis is a haunting six note series of clear ascending and descending whistle notes. While not loud, the pitch of the song enables it to carry for more than a mile, thus lending to its haunting quality.

HABITAT: The Mystērium Rara Avis lives in brushy areas in the vicinity of Eastern Washington's apple orchards. They are elusive birds in that they rarely venture out from the dense underbrush where they prefer to feed and nest.

INTRIGUING TIDBIT: The song of the Mystērium Rara Avis, though rarely heard, is associated with a lifetime of good luck for the fortunate hearer.

DATE AND LOCATION SEEN:

Song for Little Bird

little bird little bird
song for little bird
do you know
your given name
little bird little
crown stripe flitter
bird powerline fruit
citrus sitting on the
tall pole ducking
into shrub-steppe
lazy flute ramble   see me
          pretty
                    pretty
          me
marking time with light
making our no sleep
guilty when the sun
turns to song familiar
human music awake
in ubiquity
repeating
your call

—Matt Gano

NORTHERN FLICKER – COLAPTES AURATUS

DESCRIPTION: The Northern Flicker is a medium-sized woodpecker, slightly larger than an American Robin. They are an eye-catching bird with a long black bill, gray head, and bright red stripe at the nape of the head or cheek. Their chests are chestnut with distinctive black dots all over, topped by a bold black bib.

VOICE: The call of the Northern Flicker is a loud "wicka-wicka-wicka."

HABITAT: Northern flickers are adaptable and can be found in a variety of habitats including woodlands and urban areas with trees. Unlike most woodpeckers, Northern flickers often forage on the ground for ants and beetles. Thus, they also like open ground in their habitat. You can find Northern Flickers in Washington year-round in large urban parks like Discovery Park in Seattle or more natural areas like Olympic National Park.

INTRIGUING TIDBIT: During the breeding season, Northern Flickers excavate cavities in trees, both live and dead, for their nests. Later, these cavities provide important habitat for other creatures, making the Northern Flicker a keystone species.

DATE AND LOCATION SEEN:

The Northern Flicker Reconsidered

If a bird could become
a poem, and why not—

promenade through wayward
stanzas, lift their couplets

of wings—what then? A high
wik-a, wik-a alchemical spell:

a cry of the private and unprintable.
Could a flicker know heartbreak?

Practice self-restraint?
Their fashion leans bold—polka dots

and stripes, bright cinnamon
to morning fog hues. The male,

handsome, with his patch of mustache.
I'd like to become their lifelong mate

should I return as a bird—a celebrated
Shad-spirit, Cotton-rump—

with the longest bird tongue
in North America.

This ode to plurality—
this epic boundless—then—

cross-stitched together
on the pages of a Northwest sky.

—Susan Rich

OLIVE-SIDED FLYCATCHER – CONTOPUS COOPERI

DESCRIPTION: The Olive-sided Flycatcher is a medium-sized bird, sized between a Sparrow and Robin. They have a long slender bill, a big head, a white throat and chest, and olive-grey wings.

VOICE: The song of the Olive-sided Flycatcher is described as sounding like "quick, three beers!" Their call is a loud series of pips.

HABITAT: Olive-sided Flycatchers prefer high trees in coniferous forests, clear cuts, and other open areas. They perch on high trees, engaging in a feeding method called "hawking" where they capture flying insects on the wing and take them back to their tree perch to eat. You'll find the Olive-sided Flycatcher in Washington late May through August, in places like the Cascade Mountains or Olympic National Park.

INTRIGUING TIDBIT: Olive-sided Flycatchers have one of the longest migration routes of all Near-Artic birds, traveling as far as Alaska to Bolivia. With such long journeys, they often arrive at their feeding grounds later than other birds, allowing them to use abandoned nests instead of building their own.

DATE AND LOCATION SEEN:

Descript: Pick Your Tears

The olive-sided fly-catcher sallies forth,
circles out, circles back. She follows up:

a bird of her word, a-type, eldest daughter.
I have never knowingly seen an olive-sided flycatcher

neither has an olive-sided flycatcher ever been recorded
seeing me. I call my mom to ask if this passerine's

on her life list. *The flycatchers are such a huge group,*
she says, *I don't even bother.* She reads to me

from a manual: "a nondescript little grey bird
with a white stomach." Then says, *you could have picked*

an easier bird. Descript: she's a seize the winged thing
kind of bird, a jeez but what a singed stage to speak from.

Descript: early researchers—thirsty men—heard her song
as "Quick, three beers!" I hear: "pick your tears."

Descript: every day I commute to school, work,
the burned out world. So much circling. Is this multiple choice?

I fill each answer in, completely, all the way to the edges.
It's true, I could have picked an easier life. Safe

to say no one has a tattoo of an olive-sided flycatcher
on the inside of their wrist but nor does an olive-sided flycatcher

have a tattoo of a human. We are even in our not-knowing.
Look at them all, wearing their white vests, so on trend.

If only I could see them from down here. If only
I was looking up instead of looking forward to the end.

—Rebecca Hoogs

PEREGRINE FALCON – FALCO PEREGRINUS

DESCRIPTION: Peregrine Falcons are crow-sized raptors with black heads, blue-gray backs, and barred white chests and bellies.

VOICE: The Peregrine Falcon can make a variety of vocalizations including a call described as sounding like "ee-chup."

HABITAT: They prefer high-up places like the cliffs of the San Juan Islands or tall buildings like the Mutual Life Building in downtown Seattle. They prey on birds, using their incredible speed to knock the bird out of the air, and follow the bird to the ground to kill and eat it.

INTRIGUING TIDBIT: Peregrine Falcons are famous for their amazing speed, able to dive at more than 200 mph. Thus they rival the cheetah as one of the fastest creatures on the planet.

DATE AND LOCATION SEEN:

When ~~Yonder~~ I Flew

When I saw the peregrine falcon peering from his mountain
perch, I thought of you. Unaware, and too young to see the
signs, your blue form stooped from its circling flight, wings
connecting Heaven and Earth. No message from the gods
would warn me, no ancient prayer could save me. Divine sage,
eternal soaring partner, we romanced the open skies, free to
live among the stars. How could we know then that one day
I would become the wanderer and you the pilgrim? And now
I seek the hallowed crack in time yearning to nest again in
those cratered lakes and castled cliffs.

—Lea Galanter

PILEATED WOODPECKER – DRYOCOPUS PILEATUS

DESCRIPTION: The Pileated Woodpecker is a mostly black, large, crow-sized bird, with a distinctive red cap and white under wing coloring.

VOICE: The laughing "keek-keek-keek-keek" call can last for a minute or more. Its drumming is also a distinctive sound, louder and more resonant than other woodpeckers. The sound is used to establish territory.

HABITAT: Found year-round in forested areas with trees large enough to support its cavity nest and supply the ants and grubs that it feeds on. This includes large urban parks like Carkeek Park in Seattle. Their search for bugs leaves behind oval-shaped gashes in the trees, evidence of their presence in the area.

INTRIGUING TIDBIT: The Pileated Woodpecker is the largest woodpecker in North America—after the extinctions of the Ivory-Billed Woodpecker and the Imperial Woodpecker.

DATE AND LOCATION SEEN:

To Do

You've planted and weeded and wheelbarrowed,
      now tapping a pencil, trying to remember
the next thing—what was it?—when a shape
      drops from the sky, shudders and stops
at a tree—red blotch—whack, whack.
      A creature big enough on this slow spring day
to make you mutter, *Ho-*
      meric, exactly like the popeyed codger
in the John Wayne flick when he sees
      how the bride and groom have broken
their bed. A big, wild woodpecker. Imagine
      how it would feel to glimpse, like this,
an ivory-billed, that one they say
      (if that's what they saw) is the last,
epic of the air, boomerang to be
      and not. But could it be
this one will make it for real?
      Make it beyond lit screens,
this pileated inkling now hopping into brisk beats
      of loopy flight. And now almost
in your grasp, the day's next thing,
      when a rattled, rising shriek riddles the air.
Again. And again you're just beginning:
      a nest of electric light, a boy
waiting for the bus and laughing
      at the cartoon bird laughing like crazy.

—Derek Sheffield

SAY'S PHOEBE – SAYORNIS SAYA

DESCRIPTION: The Say's Phoebe is a medium-sized flycatcher with a pale brownish-gray chest and darker brownish-gray heads and necks. Their bellies are a cinnamon brown.

VOICE: Say's Phoebes have a clear, slurred whistle.

HABITAT: You'll find the Say's Phoebe in open, arid areas like those found in the Columbia Basin. Look for them February through September near grasslands, canyons, and sagebrush flats.

INTRIGUING TIDBIT: Rather than drinking water directly, Say's Phoebes gain all of their hydration from the insects that they eat.

DATE AND LOCATION SEEN:

Saying Say's Phoebe

Heralder of spring, fossils date to the
late Pleistocene, cinnamon tawny chest,
long black tail that flairs; a song: *pidiweew,*
pidireep. Singing this tune in the west
of the arid, dry country—flycatcher,
weaving, sallying from perches to grab
meals in flight. Tiny assassin, feathers
slicing the wind, delicate thunderclap:
a winged thing punctuating liminal
space of land and sky. You balance the air:
looping, diving, recovering—fractal
in flight, repeating, and repeating, heir
to this realm eons before you were named,
eternal migrant vagrant, never tamed.

—Kristie Frederick Daugherty

SHRIKE
—
VIREOS
—
CORVIDS
—
SWALLOWS

AMERICAN CROW – CORVUS BRACHYRHYNCHOS

DESCRIPTION: The all-black American Crow is a medium-sized bird with outsized intelligence, able to use tools and to recognize human faces.

VOICE: The loud, descending "caaw" of the American Crow is easily recognized by nearly everyone.

HABITAT: Commonly found in urban areas, fields and forests, the American Crow is omnivorous, eating everything from fruits, seeds, and insects, to roadkill. You can find crows year-round almost anywhere. There are probably a few outside your house right now.

INTRIGUING TIDBIT: The American Crow is known for its complex social structures, with juveniles helping to raise younger siblings and communal gatherings of up to 10,000 birds on cold winter nights. Crows also hold rituals for their dead, one of only three bird species known to conduct bird funerals.

DATE AND LOCATION SEEN:

The Crows Start Demanding Royalties

Of all the birds, they are the ones
who mind their being armless most:
witness how, when they walk, their heads jerk
back and forth like rifle bolts.
How they heave their shoulders into each stride
as if they hoped by some chance
new bones there would come popping out
with a boxing glove on the edge of each.

Little Elvises, the hairdo slicked
with too much grease, they convene on my lawn
to strategize for their class action suit.
Flight they would trade in a New York minute
for a black muscle car and a fist on the shift
at any stale green light. But here in my yard
by the Jack-in-the-Box Dumpster
they can only fossick in the grass for remnants

of the world's stale buns. And this
despite all the crow poems that have been written
because men like to see themselves as crows
(the head-jerk performed in the rearview mirror,
the dark brow commanding the rainy weather.)
So I think I know how they must feel:
ripped off, shook down, taken to the cleaners.
What they'd like to do now is smash a phone against a wall.
But they can't, so each flies to a bare branch and screams.

—Lucia Perillo

BARN SWALLOW – HIRUNDO RUSTICA

DESCRIPTION: The acrobatic Barn Swallow is a small graceful bird with a dark-blue head and body with cinnamon underparts. They have a deeply-forked tail with white spots.

VOICE: The Barn Swallow's song is a series of cheerful chirps, squeaks and trills. Their call is a soft and pleasant "wit-wit."

HABITAT: : In the spring and summer, open areas like lakes, agricultural fields, and other farmland attract Barn Swallows as they seek insects to eat. As their name implies, the Barn Swallow is comfortable with human habitations like barns and bridges, where they build their cup-shaped mud nests in small colonies with 4-6 other Barn Swallows.

INTRIGUING TIDBIT: Barn Swallows eat an incredible number of flies, mosquitoes, and other insects—making them natural pest controllers. A single Barn Swallow can eat hundreds of insects a day.

DATE AND LOCATION SEEN:

aerialists

the facile
grace of them
at dusk the silken arcs of barnswallows

~

from the eaves
from the mud nest-cups
a famished chee-chee-chee

~

from barnlight
drawing their shadows like threads
swallows go sewing stars to the trees

—Andrew Robin

BLACK-BILLED MAGPIE – PICA HUDSONIA

DESCRIPTION: The Black-billed Magpie is a crow-sized bird, mostly black, with white chest and white and iridescent blue-green wing feathers that flash when they fly. They possess piercing red eyes. Like their corvid relatives the crow and the jay, Black-billed Magpies are social birds. They form family flocks of 6–10 birds and engage in communal roosting during non-breeding seasons.

VOICE: The vocal, Black-billed Magpie makes a loud raucous call.

HABITAT: Black-billed Magpies are found in Eastern Washington in a wide variety of habitats including farmlands, wetlands, woodlands, and urban areas. Look for these birds year-round in the Yakima Valley or Columbia National Wildlife Refuge.

INTRIGUING TIDBIT: The nest of a Black-billed Magpie is a large domed structure that can last for 4 or more years. They are often reused by other bird species.

DATE AND LOCATION SEEN:

Charmed

Some thought they said, *Pie, pie.*
A caw that rachets from fenceposts
(not enough *cuss* in raucous) if ever

the wind delivers a whiff of decay
(when they aren't filching kibble
or snatching ground nestlings).

Egg slurpers. Vulturous appetite
all gussied up in undertaker pallor
for formal dining. Carcass dancers.

Their black gleams oil-spill iridescence,
the obsidian of a hearse. Sideways
glancers. Their white the white of bones

pecked clean. Roadkill comforters.
A swoon of ants, a trance of flies
have set the table for these

gristle wrestlers to hold council
(we call it a charm). We called
that meadow/crime scene The Island

because Simcoe Creek formed
a question mark on three sides. Bone
pickers, whose pallbearers are you?

—Allen Braden

CLARK'S NUTCRACKER – NUCIFRAGA COLUMBIANA

DESCRIPTION: The Clark's Nutcracker is a compact, jay-sized bird with a gray body and black wings with white patches. They have a white eye ring and white tail feathers. They have long sharp bills.

VOICE: The call of the Clark's Nutcracker is a loud, harsh "kraaa."

HABITAT: The Clark's Nutcracker prefers open pine forests in mountainous regions in higher elevations. While they are in Washington year-round, they are most easily seen in the summer and fall when they are gathering and storing seeds. Look in places like the subalpine areas of the Mount Baker-Snoqualmie National Forest or in white bark pine stands in the Okanogan-Wenatchee National Forest.

INTRIGUING TIDBIT: It takes remarkable spatial memory for the Clark's Nutcracker to retrieve the up to 30,000 pine seeds that they store each season. They also have a special throat pouch that allows them to carry more than 90 pine seeds at once. Their seed caching practice also makes them vital to supporting forests by dispersing and planting pine seeds.

DATE AND LOCATION SEEN:

Mapmaker

Whenever I see
a stand of whitebark pine—
solitary or sturdy in tight bands
high on an alpine ridge—

I think of the seed cache
from which it leaped
into being, the time it takes
a nutcracker to pry open

a fresh cone, stash
a passel of nuts
in loose volcanic earth
yellowing now in yesterday's

sunlight like a map
in a nutcracker's mind.
If most seeds stir
site specific memory,

devoured like a winter storm,
still that leaves a handful
to stake out bygone
claims, saplings sprung

in a spindle of needles.
Oh, gray distinction flashing
black wings at the treeline,
raking the air with brash

hurrahs—come to this clearing
seen or unseen—
ward then warden of
the creeping pine

or that light that thrives
on lapse exactly—
memory's keeper
in a forest of forgetting.

—Kevin Craft

Hiroko

COMMON RAVEN – CORVUS CORAX

DESCRIPTION: The Common Raven is a large, all-black songbird known for keen intelligence and problem-solving skills. They have a thick curved bill, shaggy throat feathers and, in flight, their tail feathers form a wedge shape.

VOICE: While the raven has over 30 different vocalizations, they are most known for a deep croaking sound. They are also able to mimic sounds in their environments including human speech.

HABITAT: Found in nearly all parts of the state except urban areas, ravens can be seen soaring over open fields, forests, mountains, or coastal areas. In addition to eating insects and fruit, they hunt small animals or scavenge carrion. They also enjoy dining at dumps like the one in Yakima.

INTRIGUING TIDBIT: In the urban parts of Washington, if you see a big black bird, you are likely seeing a crow. It can be challenging to tell the difference, but ravens are larger with bigger beaks. Crows travel in groups while ravens tend to be alone or in pairs, rarely flocking together in a "conspiracy."

DATE AND LOCATION SEEN:

An Unkindness of Ravens

I'm still not used to the way they converse
on the rooftops of my new neighborhood
amid raised voices and the smell of bacon.
Audible for more than a mile they're not afraid
to make their presence known, to *kraa*
"I'm here" to their cronies. Ravens are gutsy,
sure of themselves. Nothing about them
is pretty or timid, not their monochromatic
barrel bodies, not their sharp call,
certainly not their table manners.
I've witnessed them dine on roadkill
on the boulevard below my balcony.
Car smart, they harvest a strip of intestine
then take flight inches from oncoming wheels
bloody amuse-bouche dangling from their mouths.
They range the world over, rule the roost
and mate for life while this woman,
who won't eat pig or cow or lamb, who's
afraid to speak up, sits alone with her steel
cut oats and Barry's Irish breakfast tea
pining for a good lover's spat and bacon.

—Cindy Veach

STELLER'S JAY – CYANOCITTA STELLERI

DESCRIPTION: The Steller's Jay is a striking large blue and black bird with a jaunty crest on its head. They are very intelligent birds and, like fellow corvids the crow and raven, use tools to obtain food.

VOICE: The loud voice of the Steller's Jay can be harsh and demanding, but they actually have a wide vocal repertoire. They may also mimic other birds to scare away potential threats.

HABITAT: Found year-round in forests, woodlands, and residential neighborhoods, the Steller's Jay eats almost anything including seeds, nuts, berries, insects, and even small rodents.

INTRIGUING TIDBIT: Steller's Jays are very social and are often seen in groups. They form long-term pair bonds with mates and raise their young together.

DATE AND LOCATION SEEN:

A Response 2 X Re: Changing Handle frm @J 2 @stellersjay

We, the crested corvids w/ blue and black plumage who range in the wSt frm Alaska 2 Nicaragua, have reCved Ur req 2 change our X handle frm @J 2 @stellersjay, as wL as 2 purchS Premium Membership. We must respectfully Dcline.

U suggest that our @J handle is mislEding bc usRs mIt confuse us w/ rapR LL Cool J, basketball icon Dr. J, or the Kansas Jayhawks. Nothing could B furthR frm the truth. We have worked hRd at establishing our distinctive brand of songbird and our profile photo clErly distinguishes us not only frm our lItR-hUd, shortR-legged cousins residing back Est, but also frm humans and colleg8 mascots that R neithR Bst, fish, nor fowl.

More importantly, we intend 2 retire the term "Steller's" J. Past genR8ions accepted the appell8ion as a mattR of custom, conVnience, and assimil8ion. But who was German naturalist Georg Wilhelm Steller 2 us? Mr. Steller did not "discovR" us in 1741. Our kind arrived alongside the indigenous peoples of the Americas as the ice shEts reCded. 2 our mind, Mr. Steller's contribution 2 our recognition as a speCs was submitting our cadavRs 4 taxonomic classific8ion. We may B in the vanguard of the "un-Steller" movement, but we R sure that b4 long C lions, eidRs, and C Egles will follow suit. Alas, it is already 2 l8 4 the C cow ... an Xample of how those who purport 2 "name" us also drive us in2 Xtinction. We will neithR confirm nor Dny the loc8ion of the C ape, whose killing and abduction was thwarted by Mr. Steller B ing a bad shot.

So Y @J instead of @Jay? We mIt ask U the same question. Y X and not Twitter? Y X and not "Ex" or "Eks"? It's an Sthetic choice. "J" is clEn and precise. "Jay" contains 2 Xtra lettRs 2 say the same thing. It's also practical. Y peck 3 times when 1 peck would suffice?

This also brings us 2 the pachyderm in the room. Y is Ur sales tEm pressuring us 2 purchase a Premium Membership 2 reCve the coveted blue checkmark of "verified" status? U no that we cannot make payments in anything othR than nuts, sEds, and berries. FurthRmore, U imply that if we do not buy vRifId status, U will continU 2 ignore our customR service requests 2 take down the non-consensUl videos of Js stEling eggs, Eting carrion, and mimicking hawks, small dogs, and sprinklR systems. Let us call this what it is: Xtortion. Those who pay get their "tweets" ("Xs"?) promoted, while those who don't B come victims of a campaign 2 turn the public against us.

We may appear 2 B raucous, but we remain a humble, hardworking speCs. We have no plans 2 relinquish our valUble @J handle so that U may resell it on the open market 2 the hISt bidR.

—Harold Taw

CHICKADEES

—

BUSHTITS

—

NUTHATCHES

—

CREEPERS

—

WRENS

—

DIPPER

—

KINGLETS

—

THRUSHES

AMERICAN DIPPER – CINCLUS MEXICANUS

DESCRIPTION: The American Dipper is a medium-sized songbird with a slate-gray body and brown head, white eyebrows, and a black bill. They are known for their unique ability to dive and "fly" underwater, walking along stream bottoms to search for food. They get their name from their practice of bobbing or "dipping" their bodies up and down while perched on rocks in streams.

VOICE: The call of the American Dipper is loud but musical whistled notes and trills that can be heard over the noise of a river.

HABITAT: You may find the American Dipper near swift, clear, cold mountain streams with large rocks and waterfalls. There, they forage for insects and small fish. You can find American Dippers year-round in Washington in places like Olympic National Park or Icicle Creek near Leavenworth.

INTRIGUING TIDBIT: The only aquatic songbirds, American Dippers have special adaptations for their aquatic lifestyle. This includes waterproof feathers which allow them to float like a duck. They also have a nasal flap to prevent water inhalation.

DATE AND LOCATION SEEN:

Below the Surface

Is your joy toned down by common threats
That stalk you from the prairie's tall grass
As each blade gleams in the sun's bright talons?
Does walking blue air ease your anxieties?

Song inhabits you, as do minor viruses
Squamous cell carcinoma, memory loss.
What morsel did she feed you last, before
She stepped past the nest's woven horizon?

Today, I wake and must cry out a refrain.
I wake, and this hard shell breaks inside me.
I never knew life was a precious thing
To love. I simply survived. I simply loved.

Before the note's release is a long breath.
I rise and plunge, toward algae's glowing roe.
When water's flowing shush and babble move me,
I hold the wild, free sky inside my chest.

—Paul Hlava Ceballos

AMERICAN ROBIN – TURDUS MIGRATORIUS

DESCRIPTION: A medium-sized songbird, the American Robin has a white eye ring, yellow bill, with a gray back, and rust-red breast and belly.

VOICE: The cheery, lilting song of the American Robin is one of the first heard on a spring morning, which is why the Robin is known as "the early bird."

HABITAT: We've heard that "the early bird gets the worm." That phrase is referring to the American Robin and their propensity to eat worms (and fruit and insects). Robins are found year-round in a wide range of habitats from urban neighborhoods and parks, to woodlands and open forests. Robins roost communally at night in dense vegetation.

INTRIGUING TIDBIT: Have you noticed a Robin tilting its head as it stands alert on the grass? It is listening. Yes, the American Robin can hear worms. They can also see the soil moving, indicating worms close to the surface.

DATE AND LOCATION SEEN:

Flying Under the Influence in Issaquah: A Cento

> "[American robins] get tipsy from feeding on
> fermented fruit."
> — *The Seattle Times*

The robin is the one
inside the perfect ferment:

rotten fruit
once red, now spiderspit-gray, intact but empty,

savory and bitter.
Berries, dripping with wine,

put his head into a state of chronic query.
He is all pulse and membrane

in the wobbly pirouette between song.
Cheerily, cheer up, cheer up!

Dazed, drunk, still
lurching into something—

this warm place,
this bright and restless carousel,

wings unfurled.
Cheerily, cheer up, cheer up!

Secret code of everlasting joy and sorrow,
a little project called loving the world.

—Erin Murphy

BEWICK'S WREN – THRYOMANES BEWICKII

DESCRIPTION: The Bewick's Wren is a little brown bird with a big voice. They have a long, slim bill with a slightly downward curve, a distinctive white eye stripe, gray chest and belly, and black bars on the tail feathers. Bewick's Wrens are active birds, sometimes seen hanging upside down while foraging.

VOICE: The year-round song of the Bewick's Wren is loud and penetrating. You can hear their 20 different songs in your house with all the windows closed. While many are melodious, some of their songs are harsh and raspy, and many are complex.

HABITAT: Bewick's Wrens prefer wooded and bushy areas. They like thickets and densely-planted suburban gardens where insects from plants or crevices are easy to forage.

INTRIGUING TIDBIT: The male Bewick's Wren may build several "dummy" nests before the female wren selects one to use.

DATE AND LOCATION SEEN:

Song

pronounced Buick
saucy flicky scrabbling under the limelight's

fluttering shade   sunlight filter

fast car   trilling   scolding

cocked white brow   tipped tail

crevice-loving   nest-loving   mate-for-life

chaparral & open road

cheeky songster
west of the Mississippi

our evening chime of wrens

(hidden in an eagle's plumage)
vanilla strawberry blossoms

          —Arlene Naganawa

BLACK-CAPPED CHICKADEE – POECILE ATRICAPILLUS

DESCRIPTION: The Black-capped Chickadee is a common backyard bird, found year-round in urban areas and is a regular at feeders. With its striking black cap and throat and white stripe at the cheek, this small, active bird is curious, and they love to explore their environment.

VOICE: The lively Black-capped Chickadees sing out their names with a cheery "Chica-dee-dee-dee."

HABITAT: Found throughout the state, this social bird enjoys deciduous forests, mixed woodlands, and urban or suburban environments with plenty of trees—feeding on seeds and insects in trees in small flocks of other chickadees or in mixed flocks of birds. You'll find them in any lower elevation neighborhood or city park.

INTRIGUING TIDBIT: On cold winter nights, the Black-capped Chickadee can lower their body temperature to conserve energy.

DATE AND LOCATION SEEN:

We're Here to Tell You

You don't need musicians to celebrate. Hire us,
a banditry of chickadees. *Chick a-dee-dee.*
Note the musicality of our songs

through the willows, weaving the firs. We're
bilingual, you know, quite adaptable—trading
branch for branch in deciduous or mixed forests,

drinking from your bird baths, eating at your feeders.
Our diets vary—spiders, caterpillars and such
in winter, along with berries and seeds. Come spring

we're more omnivorous, but keep your feeders full
all year, please. Note: we're especially fond
of suet and peanut butter and while we're at it,

we'd like to remind you: whether we're leftover
dinosaurs or not, you'd miss us if we were gone.

—Susan Landgraf

BROWN CREEPER – CERTHIA AMERICANA

DESCRIPTION: The tiny Brown Creeper is just like it sounds—they are brown and they creep up the sides of trees. Their mottled brown and white feathers blend so perfectly with the bark of a tree that you are unlikely to see them even when their melodious high-pitched whistle attracts your eye. Their bellies are off-white, their beaks curve downward, and they have a long stiff tail that they use for support when climbing.

VOICE: The soft high whistles of the Brown Creeper sound to some like "trees-trees-see-the-trees."

HABITAT: The Brown Creeper is found in woodlands with mature coniferous and deciduous trees. They use their long, curved beak to probe for insects, clinging with their curved claws. They spiral up a tree trunk and then fly down to start foraging on another tree.

INTRIGUING TIDBIT: The diminutive Brown Creeper only burns 4-10 calories a day. Thus, one spider can fuel 200 feet of climbing.

DATE AND LOCATION SEEN:

Invitation From One Brown Creeper to Another

Hey there,
white bellied
bark-backed neighbor.

I know
a trunk
flush to forage,

where spiders
nest, ripe
for the taking.

Seeds just
fall from
pod to beak,

and we'll
both hide
in the brown.

—Chloe Mohs

BUSHTIT – PSALTRIPARUS MINIMUS

DESCRIPTION: Bushtits are a tiny puffball of a bird, frequently traveling in cloud-like flocks. This round small bird is pale brown with a stubby bill and long tail.

VOICE: The quiet, constant call of the Bushtit often reveals their presence before you see the diminutive bird. It sounds to some like a "ts, ts, ts."

HABITAT: You can find the Bushtit in open woodlands, parks, and gardens, and places like the Yakima River Valley. They are constantly on the move, traveling in flocks of 10–40, foraging for insects and spiders. They enjoy suet at backyard feeders.

INTRIGUING TIDBIT: The Bushtit builds long sock-like nests that are up to a foot long. Unpaired males may hang out to help raise the young.

DATE AND LOCATION SEEN:

What Call Can Carry On Without its Kind

One by one by one by flock,
　　　soft gray bushtits
　　　　　　blow in
　　　　　　　　to the cherry tree.

I've never seen one sit alone for long.

　　　　　Each chest tuts: *hitherto, hitherto;*
each beak sucks insects
　　　　　from under the curls in the bark
then vacates the space it held,
a space disturbed
　　　just a touch.

　　At one time,
　　　　I might've convinced myself
that glitch in my vision was never there—
　　　　　　　　hitherto, hitherto.
　　　　Sky-dusted edges;
　　　one feathered-out cloud.

　　　　　　—Rachel Edelman

MOUNTAIN BLUEBIRD – SIALIA CURRUCOIDES

DESCRIPTION: The Mountain Bluebird is a small, brilliant-blue thrush with a round head and a straight thin bill.

VOICE: The soft voice of the Mountain Bluebird is heard prior to sunrise, as a low whistle.

HABITAT: Mountain Bluebirds prefer open areas with scattered trees including prairie and meadow edges, recently-cleared or burned areas. They forage on the ground for insects and small invertebrates, and engage in aerial hunting where they exercise their hovering skill, unique amongst bluebirds. You can find Mountain Bluebirds during their March through August breeding season in places like the alpine meadows of Mount Rainier National Park or near the nesting boxes at Joint Base Lewis-McChord.

INTRIGUING TIDBIT: The stunning blue of the Mountain Bluebird is not from pigment in their feathers. It comes from light scattering through their feather structure.

DATE AND LOCATION SEEN:

The Blue Rumor

I just heard a twittered "few" and then a sweet "chur chur"
Oh sweetheart, they're calling us the "BlueBirds of Happiness"
murmuring we bring reverie—Hmmm, we can live with that,
right darlin'? Just call us *Sialia currucoides*.

We do choose to live high, (happiness here!) close to 10,000 feet up,
where it's wild and wondrous, spacious and spare.
The little lady, blue, (but not as blue as her old man)
chose me for her guy 'cause my place is safely situated, secluded.

This year I picked a nest box. She likes it better than the old
pecker hole we lived in last year, too many visitors.
It's her job to decorate and she does have a way with pine needles
and straw. While she builds the nest, I ward off bullies.

My wife lays the most perfect eggs, pale blue or white, 4 or 5 of 'em.
Precious little fellas, we both protect the heck out of them.
A couple weeks later, crack, and we're parents of hungry mouths.
Now, I'm either hovering or takin' flycatching flights for insects.

Yep, the insects are delish in summer. In winter, berries
are mighty satisfying. We even eat mistletoe—taking
the pressure off during the season of kissing. We devour
juniper berries, elderberries and grape seeds too. Tasty.

So, I guess the rumors are true. Come sing with us at dawn.

—Beverly Fesharaki

RED-BREASTED NUTHATCH – SITTA CANADENSIS

DESCRIPTION: The Red-breasted Nuthatch's black cap, white eyebrow, and black eye line gives them a bandit-like look, compounded by their habit of creeping down a tree while other birds typically work their way up trees to feed. A small, active bird, the Red-breasted Nuthatch is found year-round in coniferous forests.

VOICE: The nasally "yank, yank" of the Nuthatch is slow and steady, often continuing for a minute or more.

HABITAT: The Nuthatch prefers conifer forests where they find insects and seeds in tree bark. They are also known to enjoy sunflowers and suet in the backyard feeders of homes near mature forests.

INTRIGUING TIDBIT: The Red-breasted Nuthatch mixes an insect-repelling resin from conifer sap to repel predators and insects.

DATE AND LOCATION SEEN:

Small But Sturdy

The Red-breasted Nuthatch is a Wednesday kind of bird.
No Saturday flash or bold like a Monday. This small
mid-week parade of a bird with its tin trumpet call

has a knuckled big toe so it can march headlong down
any tree with rough bark and crevices, one of the only birds
    to do so.
Four inches long with a rusty belly. And they're monogamous.

One big love with a sprinkle of drama: he woos her by dancing
wings-out with a side sway. She likes a good dancer. She likes
him near and will sound her trumpet nonstop if he strays too far.

They work together to build their nest, store seeds, share
    childcare,
winter in place. Some live over seven years, blue-zone birds.
As for me, forty years married, thirty years in the same house.

So many storms have shaken my nest. I watch the nuthatches
plunge headfirst, finding bits of treasure no one else can see.

—Michele Bombardier

RUBY-CROWNED KINGLET – REGULUS CALENDULA

DESCRIPTION: Ruby-crowned Kinglets are small, rotund songbirds with olive-green coloring, white eye rings, and white wing bars. The male possesses a red crest that he usually keeps hidden but can raise when excited. They are very active, flitting through branches or even hovering to catch insects midair.

VOICE: The loud song of the Ruby-crowned Kinglet belies their small size. It starts with a few clear notes and builds to a crescendo of rapidly-paced notes.

HABITAT: Ruby-crowned Kinglets prefer wooded areas and streamside thickets but can also be found in urban areas. While they live year-round in Washington, you are more likely to see them in lowland forests, agricultural areas, and urban parks in the winter.

INTRIGUING TIDBIT: They tend to have the largest clutch of eggs relative to body size of any North American songbird.

DATE AND LOCATION SEEN:

Kinglets

in the yard early
the birds delicately
discuss what they

eat and who sees
them, their voices
scattering like seeds

—Jayne Marek

SWAINSON'S THRUSH – CATHARUS USTULATUS

DESCRIPTION: The Swainson's Thrush is a slim songbird with a round head and short straight bill. They have olive-brown backs and white eye rings, similar to their thrush relative, the American Robin. They have buff breasts with brown spots.

VOICE: The haunting song of the Swainson's Thrush is a series of reedy notes that spiral upwards.

HABITAT: You'll find the Swainson's Thrush in woodlands and parks. They tend to keep a low profile, hiding in thickets and foraging on the ground for insects and eating berries from bushes. Listen for them on spring mornings in the Snoqualmie River Valley.

INTRIGUING TIDBIT: Swainson's Thrushes migrate mostly at night. Their spring migration is relatively late and spread over a long period of time.

DATE AND LOCATION SEEN:

Letter to the Swainson's Thrush

I've grown so envious of you, little bird.

How you hatch out of tourmaline eggs

on a cup-sized pillow of green moss

woven through with ivory fungi filaments,

how your nest is a home that's soft and curative

tucked into the crook of the Alden in its thicket,

how you're russet-backed and belly-spotted,

how your eyes, buff-ringed, spectacled, stay low.

My friends and I all say how pretty you are.

I envy that, too, and how you power nap in flight.

I envy your lush life under the conifers, how

you are like these trees: so shy, that their crowns

won't ever touch. Listen: I heard your song and

though you *are* shy, I love how you sing even so.

—Jennifer Martelli

VARIED THRUSH — IXOREUS NAEVIUS

DESCRIPTION: The Varied Thrush is a stocky songbird with a striking, rich burnt-orange eyebrow stripe. Their chest and legs contrast with dark blue-gray upperparts. A black chest band completes the distinctive plumage.

VOICE: The haunting song of the Varied Thrush sounds like a fuzzy metallic whistle, each note on a different pitch.

HABITAT: Varied Thrushes keep a low profile in thick wet forests with dense understories. Like their fellow thrush, the American Robin, the Varied Thrush forages for insects on the ground. However, they prefer dense cover, only sometimes venturing into open areas. You can find them year-round in Washington, but it might be easier to see them in winter months when they venture to lower elevations, in places like Capital State Forest in Grays Harbor County.

INTRIGUING TIDBIT: The Varied Thrush is considered an indicator species for forest health, as they prefer old growth forests with patches larger than 40 acres.

DATE AND LOCATION SEEN:

Not a Sparrow

In the dream
it was not a sparrow
but a thrush, a Varied Thrush
that perched
on my sister's left foot
while she was sleeping
with her eyes open—

I thought she had died
but then saw
her chest rising—

The thrush,
was dressed in a map,
its tiny continents
drawn on deep yellow
with a fine black marker—

We were no longer home
in our ramshackle
childhood lake house
but were living
in a coastal cabin
in Oregon—

This was where the forests
had walked straight out
to the cliffs—
below which the ocean's
long lines of waves
were folding
in the glittering sunlight,
like a vast blinding grate
on the earth.

—Malena Mörling

WESTERN BLUEBIRD – SIALIA MEXICANA

DESCRIPTION: The Western Bluebird is a small thrush (related to the American Robin). They have a deep-blue head, wings, and tail, contrasting with a bold rufous breast and back.

VOICE: The song of the Western Bluebird is quiet, a series of soft warbles and chirps.

HABITAT: You'll find Western Bluebirds in open woodlands and forest edges. You might see them perching on fence wires or tree branches near open meadows where they hunt for insects. They are cavity nesters, seeking natural tree holes as well as nest boxes. Indeed, Western Bluebirds have significantly benefited from nesting box programs, like the ones at Joint Base Lewis-McChord and on San Juan Island.

INTRIGUING TIDBIT: Western Bluebirds are the least migratory of the bluebird species, with much of their migration being altitudinal rather than latitudinal.

DATE AND LOCATION SEEN:

How to Paint a Pair of Western Bluebirds

Dip your paintbrush in azure
sky, let the deepest blue swirl
over the male's wings and head,
muddle across his back feathers, throat
with sunset hues. Blend into the blood
moon streaming down his breast.

Be brave! Steep your brush
in cumulus clouds, apply impasto,
scumble toward the legs.
Eclipse each eye in obsidian.
Add graphite squiggles
for claws, legs, a modest beak.

Retrieve sunset's faded embers
for the female's chest, paint
her wings with midday haze, head
deep in early dusk. Draw a tree,
spotlight the male in a cavity nest—
no female will resist this artistry.
Anticipate sketching
four to six pale blue eggs.

—Sharon Carter

BLACKBIRDS
—
FINCHES
—
SPARROWS

AMERICAN GOLDFINCH – SPINUS TRISTIS

DESCRIPTION: The American Goldfinch, Washington's State Bird, is a small, bright yellow finch. Their black wings have white wing bars, and they also have a black forehead and tail.

VOICE: Some describe the bright, twittering call of the American Goldfinch as "po-ta-to chip!"

HABITAT: You can find American Goldfinches year-round in Washington at backyard feeders, woodlands, and open fields and meadows such as those at Discovery Park in Seattle or the Turnbull National Wildlife Refuge in Spokane county.

INTRIGUING TIDBIT: The bright yellow coloring of the American Goldfinch has earned it the nickname of "wild canary." In addition to being the state bird of Washington, The American Goldfinch is the state bird of Iowa and New Jersey as well.

DATE AND LOCATION SEEN:

Advice from a Goldfinch

It's okay to be a little dull in winter—
to be lit from the inside, except
when you're not. Wrap yourself as needed
in the grey sweater of perseverance,
let your bright yellow name fall out
in bitty tufts your body has already begun
to regenerate. We can only let go
of what we've been. And hey,
there's nothing wrong with singing
a wordless song. Spend more time
in the woods. Your family is called
a *charm*. Someday, you'll miss being able
to argue with your beloved about dinner,
about the empty feeder on the porch
and whose turn it was to fill it.
Bicker now, while you can.
Let the neighbors peep at you through
their binoculared eyes and blinds.
They wish they could be as free as you.

—Abby E. Murray

BROWN-HEADED COWBIRD – MOLOTHRUS ATER

DESCRIPTION: Brown-headed Cowbirds are small blackbirds with brown heads that contribute to their names. They possess finch-like cone-shaped bills.

VOICE: The song of the Brown-headed Cowbird sounds like whistles and low gurgles.

HABITAT: Brown-headed Cowbirds frequent fields, open meadows, forests, and urban parks with grassy areas. They also like agricultural areas and are known to follow cattle herds. You can find them year-round in the southern areas of Washington State, and from April through August throughout the state. Look for them in places like the Nisqually or Columbia National Wildlife Refuges.

INTRIGUING TIDBIT: Brown-headed Cowbirds engage in "brood parasitism" which means they lay their eggs in the nests of other bird species, leaving the other birds to raise their young. This has contributed to the decline of many forest songbirds.

DATE AND LOCATION SEEN:

How Now?

How now, Brown-headed Cow Bird? For centuries you surfed bison, munching on their bugs. But we slaughtered your rides, and you had to move on. Go West, Young Bird!

We call you "brood parasites" and not in a good way. Why make a nest when other birds will do it for you? Just fling their egg to the ground and deposit your own. Some surprised birds poke your kid's shell out; some give your egg the heave-ho. But most foster your chick because you ransack their nests if they don't.

Now you swagger around Washington State as if it's always been your home. Not many bison but so many cows. Corralled by fences and just begging to be de-bugged.

Hey, Brown-headed Cow Bird: Did you hitch a ride on my great-grandfather's wagon on the way to his homestead in Moon Creek? My grandfather moved my mother to Spokane. My father moved us farther west. Generation after generation, we made our homes in other people's nests.

—Allison Green

EVENING GROSBEAK – COCCOTHRAUSTES VESPERTINUS

DESCRIPTION: The Evening Grosbeak is a large and striking finch with bold yellow, black, and white markings. Their pale-colored, large, chunky beaks are perfect for cracking open the seeds that they like to eat. They are social birds gathering in noisy flocks, especially in winter.

VOICE: A symphony of whistles and chirps, often characterized by a loud and frequent "breet."

HABITAT: You'll find the Evening Grosbeak year-round in coniferous and mixed forests, woodlands, and semi-open country.

INTRIGUING TIDBIT: Contrary to popular belief, the Evening Grosbeak's name doesn't stem from evening singing habits. When first discovered, they were mistakenly thought to be active only in the evening, leading to their common name.

DATE AND LOCATION SEEN:

Tail, Interrupted

Some days I imagine madness and fear fell into the mixing machines, stamped my yellow bangs as furrowed brow. A beefy bill, the downswing of wings. I pretend the bards fell asleep at the wheel. Because every night "a short tail" haunts me and I'm sick of making excuses; physical descriptors were your only job. The other finches bought the business of songs and left me to raise the poems, hold high this husky neck. I know, every species must find a sacrifice: frat boy close-fisting the keg pump, Homer Simpson backstroking through buffets, then me below the forest's fringe, draining the punchbowl—with no concern for quieting the crunch or keeping clean—the bulky beggar at your feast. I'm not sure anymore who pays for sanctimony, but I know language is our only barter. I fly with black sunflower seeds still stuck to my beak and belly full and you get your gros to pronounce gross. I'm not angry. But some days I wish words were for the birds after all. Maybe then this body could've been pumped regal and round with lust. Maybe alarm for our decline is simply some off-sight thriving. Maybe my tail really is that short. Or maybe it's always been just a tail, interrupted.

—Dani Blackman

HOUSE FINCH – HAEMORHOUS MEXICANUS

DESCRIPTION: The cheerfully-social House Finch is the quintessential backyard bird, often nesting in hanging pots and frequenting feeders in family groups. With the male's stunning red head, breast and rump, it is no wonder the House Finch was once a popular cage bird.

VOICE: The loud but melodic warbling song of the House Finch is often one of the first heard in spring.

HABITAT: Found in Washington State year-round, the House Finch eats a varied diet of seeds and fruits, and berries. Highly adaptable, House Finches thrive around humans, so you can find them in any backyard or urban park like Point Defiance Park in Tacoma.

INTRIGUING TIDBIT: Male House Finches get their red coloration from the pigments in the food they eat, mainly from fruits and berries.

DATE AND LOCATION SEEN:

Hats Off to House Finches

For their ability to be everywhere—
grassland, stable, trees
along the parking strip—praise.

Praise their highly social nature
three cheers warble/ three cheers warble
little redbreast wooing.

Praise nestlings for wearing the marks
of their mothers, blurry and soft, praise
their punky featherheads.

Knotweed and thistle and sunflower's
black oil seeds: Praise bounty,
for finches aren't picky.

Their nests are stem and remnant made,
dog fur and string. Or they'll take
a move-in ready. Praise this family

living in the cardboard prefab
our child painted and brought home.
Praise the nail it hangs from

and the shady porch. Nothing fancy,
this gift, these birds. We open the spring
door carefully to avoid alarm.

—Erin Malone

HOUSE SPARROW – PASSER DOMESTICUS

DESCRIPTION: The House Sparrow is a medium-sized, stocky bird with a black bib. They are mostly gray with chestnut wings. Black stripes mark the wings and face.

VOICE: A short and frequent "cheep-cheep-cheep" call is common for the House Sparrow.

HABITAT: House Sparrows are adaptable birds that thrive in human environments including buildings in urban areas and farmlands. They are social birds and may form large flocks. They eat insects and seeds from the ground, feeders, and weed stalks. While especially visible in spring and summer, you can find House Sparrows year-round anywhere that you find people. Check out urban parks like the Westcrest Park in Seattle or places like the agricultural areas of Yakima Valley.

INTRIGUING TIDBIT: Introduced to North America in the 1850s, House Sparrows are aggressive birds that may push out native songbirds from nesting cavities or from backyard feeders.

DATE AND LOCATION SEEN:

They Met on a Telephone Line

She was a common grey-brown. He was as earthy
as a dust bath. She called, *Dee dee dee.*
He readily accepted with tremble
of heart and wing. He chose a round

kitchen vent on the second floor
corner behind a redwood's shade.
She brought dried blades of grass, thin
twigs, leaf stems, one after another.
He rattled metal, a frantic weaver's pace.

Together they attacked a purple bird
and stole mouthfuls of feathers. They finished
just before the eggs dropped between
a royal bed and her own delicate blanket.

Saliva softened flies were divided
among the open mouths. When the nest
became too small, they both waited

on a branch with bits
of caterpillar in their beaks.
The fledglings flip-flapped,
blended into bark. Quick as wind,
the four grew then soared after mates.

Without any *Farewell*, they were erased by sky.

—Carrie Albert

PINE SISKIN – SPINUS PINUS

DESCRIPTION: The Pine Siskin is a small, slender, streaky brown finch with yellow highlights on its wingtips and tail. They are very social and frequently congregate in noisy flocks.

VOICE: High-pitched "zweeeeew" and chattering chirps, warbles, and squeaks may indicate the presence of Pine Siskins.

HABITAT: You can find Pine Siskins hanging out year-round in forests, parks, and backyard gardens where they enjoy thistle feeders. They are agile feeders, sometimes hanging upside down from branch tips and pinecones to forage.

INTRIGUING TIDBIT: Pine Siskins have a variety of handy survival skills. For example, they can survive extremely cold temperatures by ramping up their metabolic rates to five times normal for several hours. They can also temporarily store seeds totaling up to 10% of their body mass in their crop, providing energy for cold nights.

DATE AND LOCATION SEEN:

Hope is the Thing

All day I've been watching them dive in and out of a makeshift
    birdbath,
a sculpture with a depression perfect for collecting rain.
    All day in the sun,
high action flitting, frenetic, alive. I reach for my binoculars,
    but my bare eyes

are enough. Their streaked bodies, their song going up the scale:
Zzzzrrrrrrrrrreeeeeeet! As the sun moves from left to right,
    purply-pink
to gray, the birds make the most of a clear, crisp day, crowd the
    perimeter,

perched in a circle I wish I could join. Hope is the thing
with wing bars. Hope is the thing with a sharply pointed bill,
yellow-edged wings, a short-notched tail, though how can I omit

that their population is down, since 1970, by 80%?
That *Allaboutbirds.com* refers to them as a *common bird*
in steep decline. Salmonella outbreaks. Prey for domestic cats,

poisoning from cyanide and DDT, from pecking at asphalt
and cement, ingesting motor oil, contaminated salt. Which is why
I'm surprised when I learn this winter we're experiencing a
    Siskin incursion,

a blizzard of siskins, yards and decks deluged. Something to do
with a lack of food up north, a southern migration in search of
    seeds,
which happens at *irregular intervals*, which happens when we
    need it most.

—Martha Silano

PURPLE FINCH – HAEMORHOUS PURPUREUS

DESCRIPTION: The Purple Finch is actually more raspberry red, the color of their head, breast, and back. They have brown wings and short, notched tails. Their bills are straight and stout like other finches.

VOICE: Purple Finches have a long, cheery-sounding musical warble with slightly slurred whistles. They also have a call that sounds like "pik, pik, pik."

HABITAT: You can find Purple Finches in the edges and open areas of forest lowlands. They forage for seeds and insects in trees and shrubs. In winter, Purple Finches are social and can flock with other finches, Pine Siskins, and other birds.

INTRIGUING TIDBIT: During the breeding season, male Purple Finches become very territorial. They show their aggression by leaning forward with necks outstretched. In courtship, they have elaborate displays which include puffing up their feathers and hopping around while singing.

DATE AND LOCATION SEEN:

feasting, at last

purple finch

such sweets   finched from across the forest:
     oilslicked sunflower   with its center silken nut
           one berry   & its tender seedheart
a slip of nectar   bedecked in petaled armor
                whole bud plundered right off the stem

from the safety of her evergreen,   this spit of red consumes
       it all—   tongues each spring
from every destination—   leaves nothing
    to fruit   to flesh into dreams

                   & so the little glutton
goes about her business   as if this were any other day   as if
   she had not defined her life   through the songs
& sutures   of people's days   the fruiting
cycle of every berry   *so tender*   *so sweet*

nothing can stop the songstealer   *raspberry-headed*
from devouring her richest fancies   *such delectable*
   delights   from admiring the crabapple
   with its rosy sheen   *supple mirror*   the deepest
satisfaction   in finding a match   of
     blush   of brightness

she sees   herself
          & bites

      —Abi Pollokoff

RED-WINGED BLACKBIRD – AGELAIUS PHOENICEUS

DESCRIPTION: The Red-winged Blackbird is a medium-sized bird with a black body and striking red and yellow shoulder patches.

VOICE: The harmonica-like trill of the Red-winged Blackbird is one of up to 18 different calls that this very social bird possesses.

HABITAT: One often sees the Red-winged Blackbird clinging to cattails in marshes, wetlands, lakes, and rivers. They are one of the most widely distributed birds in Washington and, indeed, in North America.

INTRIGUING TIDBIT: Male Red-winged Blackbirds can be very aggressive in defending their territory during breeding season. This despite the fact that they may breed with up to 15 females in a season, resulting in many of "their" nestlings being sired by other males.

DATE AND LOCATION SEEN:

Red-Winged Blackbirds

He saw them on the fence line along the dirt road to the ranch, lifting skyward, their miniscule hearts and wingbeats surmounting gravity. Their knowledge sevenfold. Seventy times seven. The birds lived free, without violation or punishment. Black plumage. Glossier in spring, less so in winter. A striking red and yellow at the shoulder. Passerine and carinate, steady and skyborne. Often, they escaped predation, but predators moved on the ground and from the sky. Snakes, mink, and wildcats, foxes, eagles, hawks. The redwings were flushed from earth to air. They dove and swooped to prevent their children from being consumed. They fled to keep from being torn asunder. What made such dynamism attainable? Who reached from heaven to earth? She glanced at him and he felt a sense of awe. Women and men walked hand in hand or alone. Like sisters. Like brothers. They died separately or together. The red-winged blackbirds flew among them, the people generally unknowing. Driven by instinct or hunger, the birds' lifespan was meager.

But their flying gladdened the sky.

—Shann Ray

VESPER SPARROW – POOECETES GRAMINEUS

DESCRIPTION: The Vesper Sparrow is a stout, medium-sized sparrow with heavy brown streaking over their off-white bodies. They have a white eye ring and their white outer tail feathers make them distinctive in flight from other similar-sized birds.

VOICE: The song of the Vesper Sparrow is a musical variety of trills.

HABITAT: You can find Vesper Sparrows from April through September in loose flocks throughout Washington's grasslands and open fields. They spend much of their time foraging for insects on the ground and they like to take dust baths. You can see males singing from higher locations such as the tops of shrubs, trees, or telephone wires. Look for them in places like the Chambers Lake area, Weir Prairie, or Scatter Creek Wildlife Recreation Area.

INTRIGUING TIDBIT: The Vesper Sparrow's name comes from their habit of singing at twilight, like the Vespers evening service sung in some churches.

DATE AND LOCATION SEEN:

Evening Song

—Pooecetes gramineus

Happy among the sedges and low grasses
overgrowing the abandoned farm,
I hop about scratching the dirt for seeds,
sometimes snag the occasional spider
fallen from its web.

Late August sky a jewel tone
as midday shadows gather.
Soon I must take to the clouds, fly south.
But for now, I'll enjoy this dry patch of earth,
puff my chest and flap my wings to make a good dirt bath.

My white eye-ring highlights my pearl black iris,
sharpens my vision
as I turn my gaze from east to west,
flash my white tail feathers, take flight.

My mate is gone,
our young have flown.
How many more Springs will I return?

Sheltered now in the high branches of a willow shrub
I sing my plaintive evening song:
"So-o long, so-o long . . .
Til next year, til next year."

—Peter Pereira

WESTERN MEADOWLARK – STURNELLA NEGLECTA

DESCRIPTION: The Western Meadowlark is a medium-sized bird with a bright yellow breast and V-shaped black bib. They have brown backs streaked in black, short tails, and long legs. Their white tail feathers flash when they fly.

VOICE: The Western Meadowlark's voice is one of its most distinctive features, with a complex melodious song of flute-like whistles followed by a musical warble. The song is very loud, often carrying more than a mile.

HABITAT: You can find the Western Meadowlark in open areas like grasslands, meadows, and agricultural fields with shrubs or fence posts for perching. They forage on the ground for insects and seeds. Look for them March through August in places like the Columbia National Wildlife Refuge, and October through March in the Kent or Cedar River Valleys.

INTRIGUING TIDBIT: The Western Meadowlark is not actually a lark. They are a member of the blackbird family and are related to grackles and orioles.

DATE AND LOCATION SEEN:

The Neglected

Sturnella neglecta

Here for the grasslands,
here for the brambled stubble fields.

Here for a scribbled, high-reaching
song. Beak breaking and entering

the meadow. Don't say
ground-feeder like it's a bad thing.

Hunger the size of a single seed
of grain. Not a soarer,

a pacer, like the worried
among us pace the dark streets.

Hunched, like a yellow-caped witch.
Here for neglect, for quietude. Folk

artist, alone in the dome-nest, built
in the hoofprint of a cow.

Gold-breasted as royalty,
but rub away the gold,

you get
Blackbird.

     —Diane Seuss

STARLING
—
WAXWINGS
—
WARBLERS

CEDAR WAXWING – BOMBYCILLA CEDROUM

DESCRIPTION: The Cedar Waxwing is a stunning bird with a sleek tan body, rakish black mask, and subtle racer crest. They have a yellow belly and waxy-looking pops of yellow and red at the wingtips. They travel in flocks, often descending en masse on fruit trees to consume all of the berries.

VOICE: The Cedar Waxwing calls with a high-pitched whistle.

HABITAT: The berry-loving Cedar Waxwing lives year-round in woodlands, orchards, and parks. While they also eat insects, they are one of the few birds that can survive only on fruit for several months.

INTRIGUING TIDBIT: The Cedar Waxwing's love of berries can get the better of them. If they gorge on overripe berries, they soon become intoxicated, tumbling from perches and crashing into objects. Fortunately, their berry high only lasts a few minutes before they begin to recover.

DATE AND LOCATION SEEN:

The Rules of Play

Years before I became a cedar waxwing,
a man ordered the pancake special

and explained my shortcomings
so adroitly I didn't have the wherewithal

to get in a word of my own.
He lifted the fork to his mouth only,

passing no berry to mine
as the waxwing male does to the female

who holds the berry in her beak
for a moment and then returns it to the male

who returns it to her who returns it to him,
courtship going on like this

until the female either swallows the berry
as prelude to the brief cloacal kiss

or just gives it back once and for all.
I love berries more than anything

and had he passed me one,
I would have devoured it immediately,

which is not how the dance goes
if dance is initiated by the waxwing,

who is so handsome, both male and female,
which means I'm beautiful now, too.

I still don't know how long it's supposed to go on,
this restraint, these exchanges.

What about appetite?
The waitress kept filling my cup,

the man kept saying things might've been otherwise
had I played at least a little hard to get.

Vagrant and without song, said to be
of "least concern," I am now an intelligent

and social bird. To attract me,
plant a blueberry bush, a juniper tree.

I'll stay until the fruit is gone.
There's a raven somewhere

who likes to slide down a snowbank
on her tail feathers then climb back up

to do it all again.
He might prefer someone like that?

Waxwings don't play games.
A game has no purpose.

The cloacal kiss is serious business.
At least no games I know,

though sometimes in winter,
members of my flock and I

eat so many fermented berries—
whatever's left on the bush—

we get a little drunk and fly erratically,
completely and incompletely sated,

like other inebriates of air.

—Catherine Barnett

EUROPEAN STARLING – STURNUS VULGARIS

DESCRIPTION: The bird that everyone loves to hate, the European Starling is actually a lovely and fascinating bird. They are black with glossy iridescent feathers that flash purple and green. They are very social and rather loud, gathering in large "murmurations" in winter.

VOICE: Starlings make a variety of squeaks, squawks, and whistles. They are also amazing mimics, imitating other birds, mechanical sounds, and even people.

HABITAT: European Starlings are very adaptable. This allows them to thrive year-round in a wide variety of habitats including urban areas, coastal areas, farmlands, open woodlands, and parks and gardens. Indeed, In Washington, they are an invasive species that aggressively competes with native birds for nesting sites.

INTRIGUING TIDBIT: European Starlings were brought to North America in 1890 as part of a plan to bring all birds mentioned in Shakespeare's works to Central Park. "Nay, I'll have a starling shall be taught to speak / Nothing but 'Mortimer,' and give it him / To keep his anger still in motion." *Henry IV, Part 1.*

DATE AND LOCATION SEEN:

Carmen from *Mozart's Starling*

Carmen imitates the coffee grinder—an unpleasantly loud but accurate *Whirrrrraaaaah!*—when I open the jar of coffee beans and pour them into the machine. Every evening, I walk into the kitchen to grind the beans for the next morning. There is Carmen, eager to announce, first the ker-klunk of the coffee-jar lid as I set it on the counter, then *Whiirrrraaaaah!* When I open the microwave door, she immediately interjects her eerily mechanical, *Beep! Beep-beep!* And the wine vacuum sound? when she hears the clink of the bottle.

All of this made me realize, like these household sounds, the words she imitates are not called out at random. When I come downstairs in the morning, it is not the microwave sounds or the kissing I hear first, but the greeting, *Hi Carmen! Hi Carmen! Hi Carmen!*—the first words I say to her each day. And when I stop to peek into her aviary? *C'mere.* All participatory, *anticipatory* of what is going on aurally in her world and what precipitates what. She is basically saying, *I know what's going on! I am part of this!* I am filled with wonder. And with questions.

—Lyanda Lynn Haupt

WILSON'S WARBLER – CARDELLINA PUSILLA

DESCRIPTION: The Wilson's Warbler is a small yellow bird with a distinctive black cap. In some light they can appear more green than yellow.

VOICE: You'll hear the Wilson's Warbler make a series of chirps that increase in speed and volume.

HABITAT: Sometimes known as the "thicket warbler," the Wilson's Warbler prefers dense, moist, shrubby cover like willow and alder thickets. There, they forage actively for insects, constantly moving and flicking their tails nervously.

INTRIGUING TIDBIT: The Wilson's Warbler is named for Alexander Wilson, the "father of American ornithology."

DATE AND LOCATION SEEN:

Margin of Error

Tip of the skull cap, black
hole in a blaze of olive sunlight
scavenging among leaves,
scourge of insects on the fly—

there's one at my window
twitching like a weather eye—poll
of one sporting no opinion,
miracle of circumstance in May—

which is to say
how does he find his way to our backyard
year after year (reiterating
emigré) ransacking the lilac,

pillaging the mock orange—light
weight (six or seven grams)
precipitate of the Pacific
flyway come to call one day here

a wilderness (I am that I am)
only to disappear beneath his cursory cap
in sympathy with darkness
as with archives, trafficking in previous lives.

—Kevin Craft

YELLOW-RUMPED WARBLER – SETOPHAGA CORONATA

DESCRIPTION: Yellow-rumped Warblers are medium-sized birds with bright yellow patches on the chest and rump. They are otherwise gray, black, and white.

VOICE: The song of the Yellow-rumped Warbler is a clear, warbled, and variable trill.

HABITAT: Yellow-rumped Warblers prefer open areas with shrubs and scattered trees, secondary forests, agricultural and residential areas. Look for them in parks and residential areas or the coniferous forests of the Cascade Mountains.

INTRIGUING TIDBIT: The nickname of the Yellow-rumped Warbler is "butter-butt."

DATE AND LOCATION SEEN:

Yellow-rumped Warblers

Each spring they use the tender underbelly
of night to travel the Mississippi flyway,

steady their hearts and wings for the journey.
The new season of small stars is their roadmap,

and all the skies they've known are tucked inside
them, streaked with contrails and noctilucent clouds.

They contain the places themselves, each berry
or seed, the sounds of water, its chir or chatter,

the slight lights of suspicion near each house.
The yellow-rumped warblers mark the peak

of spring, the time of year in which I was born.
And though I wasn't technically an orphan,

I was given up for adoption at three days old,
the cord that tied me to one mother was cut

and proffered to another. Of course
there were excuses, profound reasons to be given

away. I blame no one. On windy days
my neighbor would fly a flag that mimicked the beating

of wings. And I always felt confused.
Everyone loves the yellow-rumps,

the mottled black and white bodies
punctuated with bright bits of cloisonne gold,

the sharp *cheks* they make while
flying and foraging, calling as they

change direction. How many times did I fear
the same fate? As her, I mean. The relief at the sight

of blood each month. To know the burden
like the dampness of dusk would not be mine

this time. And though I didn't know
who I came from for years,

I wore a certain shame that was as thick
as the brush at the canopy's edge

where yellow-rumped warblers sally out
to catch their food. These birds have adapted

to eat almost anything to survive
the long winters. In reality, they may migrate;

they may not. What images from her life
might be alive in me? The twisted dead deer along

an Ohio highway? The lightening that skeletons
across the night sky? The dusting of dandelions

against a newly green yard? The flashes of yellow
that mark the end of a cold lonely season?

—Didi L. Jackson

Hiroko

NATIVE SPARROWS
—
WESTERN TANAGER
—
LAZULI BUNTING

DARK-EYED JUNCO – JUNCO HYEMALIS

DESCRIPTION: The Dark-eyed Junco is a small sparrow with a dark colored head, a gray or brown body, and white belly. The bird's white outer tail feathers flash distinctively in flight.

VOICE: The Dark-eyed Junco's song is a long, pleasant trill but they also make a distinctive ticking sound to signal alarm. Other birds will frequently flee upon hearing the junco's alarm call.

HABITAT: Found year-round in forests and woodlands, as well as in more urban parks and backyards. Look for them in places like Discovery Park in Seattle. As ground feeders, they will kick at the ground to uncover seeds and insects. They will also dine at or under bird feeders.

INTRIGUING TIDBIT: The Dark-eyed Junco is a social bird with a rigid social hierarchy. You might observe dominant birds chasing less dominant birds away from your feeder.

DATE AND LOCATION SEEN:

March

to the juncos

I offer to your black hoods
unconditional surrender

this makeshift prayer
part bandage   part apology

here eat   here bathe
only endure   we can't go back

can't unstack the errors
I'm orchestrating days

to a score I can't decipher
no one is in charge

what will be reckless
in retrospect?   can I

like the dark-eyed junco   be
satisfied   with what I find scattered

on the ground   I rinse my hands
rinse again   hair and thoughts

equally unkempt   I fever
my gaze to the window

like a lover craving hourly
rendezvous   envy

your untroubled habit
your forage   flock   flight

—Elizabeth Austen

GOLDEN-CROWNED SPARROW – ZONOTRICHIA ATRICAPILLA

DESCRIPTION: Golden-crowned Sparrows are large sparrows with a black cap topped by a yellow stripe or crown. They have brown backs with black streaks and their chests and bellies are gray. Their cone-shaped bill is darker on the top than the bottom.

VOICE: Some describe the three-note whistle of the Golden-crowned Sparrow as sounding like "oh-dear-me."

HABITAT: You can find Golden-crowned Sparrows in the winter in bushy areas, thickets, and gardens where they forage on the ground for seeds, fruits, and insects. You may find them in mixed flocks with other sparrows.

INTRIGUING TIDBIT: The Golden-crowned Sparrow sometimes mates with the White-crowned Sparrow, creating interesting hybrid birds.

DATE AND LOCATION SEEN:

Golden Diva

No bigger than a puff
of dandelion fluff, round bobbin
on a bare twig, breast
of muted light, gold-daubed head,
beak and feet tucked tight,
wings wrapped against wind.

Reflected in a puddle, upside down, crowned
by cumulous clouds, imbiber
of dew and seeds, tiny diva,
rouged beauty hopping branch
to water, and back.

—Bethany Reid

LAZULI BUNTING – PASSERINA AMOENA

DESCRIPTION: Lazuli Buntings are colorful birds with a sky-blue head, cinnamon chest, and flanks; they have a white belly and white wing bars.

VOICE: The song of the Lazuli Bunting is a series of high-pitched musical notes.

HABITAT: You'll generally find Lazuli Buntings east of the Cascades. There, they prefer open brushy areas and shrub areas near open grasslands where they can forage for insects and seeds on the ground. Look for them during their breeding season late spring through summer in places like the Columbia River Gorge or Okanogan-Wenatchee National Forest.

INTRIGUING TIDBIT: Each male Lazuli Bunting has only a single song, but he makes up his own unique song by rearranging the syllables of their base song and combining it with song fragments from other males.

DATE AND LOCATION SEEN:

The Shape of Light

Color is a verb—I remember as he spikes
tips of neck feathers, leans his head back, flashes
shades of blue, turns syrinx to song. Snag of sky,

and like the sky, a trick that's empty
of pigment, just a bend our eyes see as gemstone,
shallow sea, throat of northern lights, turquoise traded

from another world. We sit together on a ledge
of sandstone—my mother's sit-spot, a slope of scrub oak
and sumac below the hogbacks, those slabs of stone that anchor

us home. In this song neighborhood, each male sings his
    signature
of rivered notes, a question he asks and answers his whole life,
over and over, singing *this*, this cup of rootlets and grass,

these four blue eggs, this tending. Later, they'll fly in starlit
currents south. They'll stop and gather and molt every feather,
    grow
new blue in what is called a mural or a sacrifice.

On her fused foot bones and metal knee, my mother walks slowly
down the trail. Blue is a verb, a hood of bright grief,
sheer refusal of grief. Even buried in darkness,
a color made of sunlight—in starlight, a memory of blue.

—Anne Haven McDonnell

SAGEBRUSH SPARROW – ARTEMISIOSPIZA NEVADENSIS

DESCRIPTION: Sagebrush Sparrows are medium-sized, brownish-gray birds with white eye rings and a white mustache stripe. They possess a dark spot on their otherwise light-colored breast. They have relatively long tails, dark-colored with light edges, which they flick when they run.

VOICE: The Sagebrush Sparrow's song is abrupt and lively, with patterns and frequencies that carry well in the open landscape that they prefer.

HABITAT: Not surprisingly, Sagebrush Sparrows prefer arid shrublands and grasslands as well as open areas with scattered shrubs. They spend most of their time on the ground or in dense shrubs foraging, running, and hopping about with tails raised. Look for them from spring to early summer in the Moses Coulee.

INTRIGUING TIDBIT: Adapting to their arid habitat, Sagebrush Sparrows get most of their water from their food.

DATE AND LOCATION SEEN:

Ode to the Sagebrush Sparrows Spotted Off-Road
on the Old Vantage Highway

the old road   studded w/bunch grass scrub-steppe
silver-blue clumps   above the river

          below blue   sky   along the gorge

spiders rustle   wind brushes up

                    Dear Sagebrush Sparrows—

Dear Bird of Concern

          your numbers low and going missing

but still   in February you show up   in pairs

dear bird, dear bird of concern

                    do you know there are federal files on you—?

                    —Jeanne Morel

SONG SPARROW – MELOSPIZA MELODIA

DESCRIPTION: The Song Sparrow is a medium-sized sparrow. They have streaked brown and white plumage with a dark brown spot on the chest. They sport a brown cap over a gray face.

VOICE: Song Sparrows are known for their melodious and complex songs which consist of a varying series of clear notes, trills, and repeated phrases.

HABITAT: The most abundant sparrow in the region, you can find Song Sparrows year-round in nearly any wooded environment near water. This includes brushy fields, marshes, wetlands, parks, and suburban gardens. They feed on the ground, using a hopping double-scratch method to expose seeds.

INTRIGUING TIDBIT: During the breeding season, male Song Sparrows sing up to every 8 seconds, averaging over 2,300 songs in a single day.

DATE AND LOCATION SEEN:

Song Sparrows in Winter

They come to peck on the ground under the feeders,
    scratching for seeds the finches sloppily kick & spill.

W/ little striped heads, little striped chests, they linger in
    salal, in the wintering ninebark, barely visible, same

brown as the branches, fluffed against the wind. Song sparrows
    like their own kind the most, lifting in scared groups,

then on the snow together, finding tiny bits to eat, raising
    their bright chirp/chips, hi hi hi's, buzzes, whistles.

Song sparrows were once prized as delicacies & eaten
    by royalty & common people alike. The birds foraging

on the snow in Bruegel's iconic *Winter Landscape with a Bird Trap*
    are often described as sparrows—in the painting

an old door propped on a stick teeters above feeding birds.
    Imagine the chirps, a bite to the wind. Winter 1564

recorded as the hardest in memory, the birds & trap added late
    to Bruegel's composition, apparently for what

must be a nod to appetite & need, humans like song sparrows
    scraping for even the smallest things to stay alive.

—Katharine Whitcomb

SPOTTED TOWHEE – PIPILO MACULATUS

DESCRIPTION: Spotted Towhees are large sparrows with black hood, back and tail. They have white spots on their wings, a white belly, and rusty red flanks. They have deep red eyes.

VOICE: The Spotted Towhee makes a variety of sounds including a mew that sounds like a cat and a song that sounds like "drink-your-tea."

HABITAT: A ground forager, you'll find the Spotted Towhee in shrubby sections of forests, wetland edges, and residential areas. With their distinct and noisy two-footed foraging method, you often hear the Spotted Towhee before you see them. You can find Spotted Towhees year-round in Washington in places like Spokane's Riverside Park.

INTRIGUING TIDBIT: Rather than flying away, the Spotted Towhee tends to run away from danger.

DATE AND LOCATION SEEN:

Visitor

The spotted towhee walks cautiously around the feeder
then hops back in the bushes. Not the right kind of seed,
I guess. Insects are flitting about the leaves. Oh, little bird,
your name has changed from rufous-sided to spotted but
the first rolls off the tongue like limoncello, the other a
stutter of white flakes. Who are those that keep changing
our names until we can't remember our own language?

—Cynthia Pratt

WESTERN TANAGER – PIRANGA LUDOVICIANA

DESCRIPTION: The Western Tanager is a small bird with a bright red head, bright yellow body, and striking black wings with light-colored bars. They look surprisingly tropical for the Pacific Northwest.

VOICE: You could mistake the Western Tanager's song for that of an American Robin. However, the Tanager's song is faster and hoarser.

HABITAT: The Western Tanager lives May through September in open coniferous forests and woodlands. They eat a variety of insects including bees and grasshoppers.

INTRIGUING TIDBIT: The red pigment on the male Western Tanager's face comes from their diet—an insect that feeds on conifer trees.

DATE AND LOCATION SEEN:

Song Canopy

What do you call a flame with wings?
Brilliant yellow with a sunset head,
establishing territory with nonstop singing.
How would the world change
if we claimed our homes with music?

Arriving in the dark, in the spring,
in the morning their gold feathers land
on one tree in the canopy:
musical notes,
drops of butter,
coins falling from the sky.

Females prepare for the next generation,
scaffold and floor, grasses and moss:
blue-green, spotted moons
hatch, helpless.
Without her, the species would not survive.
The oldest wild one recorded lasted 7 years.
What were you doing 7 years ago?

When all around you seems lost,
keep your eyes turned up
toward the canopy.
Listen for the singing.
You can create
a whole new life in seven years
that doesn't yet exist.

—Kristie McLean

WHITE-CROWNED SPARROW – ZONOTRICHIA LEUCOPHRYS

DESCRIPTION: The bright black and white cap of the White-crowned Sparrow makes them easy to pick out from their "little brown bird" brethren. They have a gray body and white streaked brown wings and bright yellow beak.

VOICE: The persistent song of the White-crowned Sparrow is distinctive with a two-part whistle followed by some trills. The song might be heard as "seee pretty-pretty meee."

HABITAT: The White-crowned Sparrow lives in open and shrubby habitats including forest edges, weedy fields, parks, and backyards. They forage on the ground, using a "double scratch" hop that is similar to the Spotted Towhee.

INTRIGUING TIDBIT: White-crowned Sparrows can engage in unihemispheric slow wave sleep. This allows them to stay partially awake for up to 2 weeks during migration.

DATE AND LOCATION SEEN:

What Does Her Song Cost?

"A woman needs a man like a bird needs a bicycle," my T-shirt says, and surely that sparrow is wearing a bike helmet. White-crowned perched on rabbitbrush that spills from a bowl of lava columns stacked like mismatched cans.

This west-coast state often splits down the mountains. Your coast-side White-crowned hangs out year-round in urban sprawl, begs at your sidewalk café, snatches your French fry, her fat grub.

East of the Cascades she sings a different dialect. Different subspecies. Homesteaded on Denali this summer, wrapping her loves in willow twig and marmot fur, flew 1600 miles from those Northern Lights to these Columbia River shrubs. Does her song swell with arctic seeds, bighorn hooves dodged, grizzly stripping life from a fawn? Does her song praise winter sun, joys of the flock?

The female White-crowned sings, yes. Her song, softer and more nuanced than his, challenges invaders and strengthens the pair's monogamous bond.

My friend loaned an exchange student a bike, and it was love: the girl delighted in wind on her face, like flying, in wearing nothing on her head—sneakily stripped off the helmet when alone. Then vanished one day into Canada. Carrying all her own secrets. Her silence a wisdom that breaks my heart. Left behind in jumbled questions and broken trust, we hold hope her escape transcends its endless price.

While the ancestral female sang, in about a third of bird species, females have fallen silent. Speaking for myself, which I too often don't, silence is the gateway betrayal.

What is the cost of a voice to a female? ornithologists ask. And what is the cost of a female's voice to her nest?

"How can I ke-ee-p from singing?" lilts the White-crowned, as sunlight catches golden seeds, cheatgrass snaked with barbed wire, and breaths of sage. Up she flits, her voice hanging in the air behind her.

—Jaqueline Haskins

GRAY CATBIRD – DUMETELLA CAROLINENSIS

DESCRIPTION: The Gray Catbird is a medium-sized songbird with a gray body, black cap, and black tail feathers. They also have a chestnut patch under their tail feathers.

VOICE: Gray Catbirds have a wide variety of vocalizations. Similar to a Mockingbird, their song may include imitations of other birds, frogs, or mechanical sounds—going for several minutes without repetition. Their call, however, is the source of their name, sounding to some like a harsh cat's mew.

HABITAT: It can be hard to find the Gray Catbird, as they like to skulk in dense undergrowth and thickets. They prefer streams with thick, low growth, and woodland edges. Additionally, they are only present May through September in Eastern Washington. Look for them in river valleys like the Yakima or the Okanogan.

INTRIGUING TIDBIT: Gray Catbirds are important insect predators and help control pests like gypsy moths.

DATE AND LOCATION SEEN:

Prayer for the Catbird's 5th Quill—

the longest quill, part of a set of gray feathers
that lifts and carries the catbird over leafy thickets, along edges
of woods and streams, swamps
and brush fields to the backyard feeder
where I lure you with mealworms for your whistle and trill,

notes you steal from the goldfinch and wren.
In the middle of a melody,
you sample the croak of a frog, mimic
a doorbell, or squawk like an unoiled hinge
for the sheer joy of sound.

In summer I listen to you sing, late
into the evening. Your eponymous cat's meow,
orchestrated with ringtones and the ratchet
of a windup toy, an intricate improvisation
that will never be repeated.

Those who say your color is drab
haven't seen the shine of your black cap
when you bow in the thorn scrub to attract a mate.
Blue-gray under gray, wings drooped, tail raised,
you reveal your cinnamon patch.

May you never be bred in an aviary.
May you attack a snake with fury.
May you move and glide with grace.
May your cadences never falter.

—Jennifer Markell

Traveling

Light "propagates"
(as in propaganda?),

meaning it clones itself
to travel.

＊

There are flame shapes
in the wood grain
now

＊

The birds I thought
were chickadees
may have been nuthatches.

We name things
to know where we are.

—Rae Armantrout

GLOSSARY

Altitudinal Migration: A type of migration where birds move between higher and lower elevations, rather than north and south. This is a behavior of the Western Bluebird.

Brood Parasitism: A reproductive strategy where one species lays its eggs in the nests of another species, leaving the host to raise the young. This is practiced by the Brown-headed Cowbird.

Carrion: The decaying flesh of dead animals. This is a primary food source for Turkey Vultures and a secondary one for Common Ravens.

Covey: A small group or flock of birds, especially partridges or quail. California Quail gather in large coveys.

Crepuscular: Being active primarily during twilight. Common Nighthawks are crepuscular.

Dabbling Duck: A duck that feeds by tipping forward in the water and reaching for food on the surface or in shallow water. Examples include the Cinnamon Teal, Mallard, and Northern Shoveler.

Diurnal: Being active primarily during the day. The Snowy Owl is a diurnal hunter.

Diving Duck: A duck that dives underwater to find food. Examples include the Bufflehead, Common Goldeneye, and Ring-necked Duck.

Estuary: A coastal body of water where freshwater from rivers mixes with saltwater from the ocean. Many birds can be found in estuaries, including the Northern Shoveler, Snow Goose, Least Sandpiper, Marbled Godwit, and Dunlin.

Gallinaceous Birds: An order of ground-dwelling birds that include chicken-like birds such as quail.

Hawking: A hunting method where birds capture flying insects in the air and take them to a perch to eat. Olive-sided Flycatchers use hawking.

Indicator Species: A species whose presence, absence, or abundance reflects the overall health of an ecosystem. The Dunlin, Northern Spotted Owl, and Varied Thrush are all considered indicator species.

Irruption: A sudden, irregular movement of a large number of birds moving much farther south than usual. This behavior is demonstrated by Snowy Owls.

Kleptoparasitism: A feeding behavior where one animal steals food from another. American Coots engage in kleptoparasitism.

Magnetoreception: The ability to detect magnetic fields, used by some animals for navigation. Rock Pigeons use magnetoreception for navigation.

Monogamous: Having only one mate at a time. Canada Geese, Ospreys, and Northern Spotted Owls are monogamous.

Murmuration: A large flock of starlings that fly in synchronized, swirling patterns. European Starlings gather in large murmurations in winter.

Nocturnal: Being active primarily at night. The Black-crowned Night Heron and Barred Owl are primarily nocturnal, while the Common Nighthawk is not strictly nocturnal.

Omnivorous: Eating both plants and animals. The Glaucous-winged Gull and American Crow are omnivores.

Preen Gland: A gland near the tail that produces oil that birds use to waterproof their feathers. The Double-crested Cormorant has less preen oil than other birds, and the Northern Flickers preen themselves with ant remains, which contain a type of acid that kills parasites.

Raptor: A bird of prey with sharp talons and a hooked beak. Examples include the Bald Eagle, American Kestrel, and Peregrine Falcon.

Syrinx: The vocal organ of birds, located at the base of the trachea. Turkey Vultures lack a syrinx.

Unihemispheric Slow Wave Sleep: The ability to sleep with one half of the brain while the other half remains active. White-crowned Sparrows engage in this behavior.

UV Vision: The ability to see ultraviolet light, which allows some birds to track prey. American Kestrels can see UV light.

Winnowing: A sound created by a bird's feathers during flight. Wilson's Snipes make a winnowing sound.

RESOURCES

ADDITIONAL FIELD GUIDES & BOOKS

- *National Geographic Field Guide to the Birds of North America* by Jon L. Dunn and Jonathan Alderfer
- *Birds of the Puget Sound Region: Coast to Cascades* by Dennis Paulson, Bob Morse, Tom Aversa and Hal Opperman
- *Pacific Northwest Birding Companion* by Stan Tekiela

MOBILE APPS

- Audubon Bird Guide—This app includes descriptions, photos, and sounds of birds. The Bird ID feature walks you through the process of identifying a bird. It also has features for logging sightings. Audubon.org/app
- eBird (Cornell Lab of Ornithology)—Participate in citizen science by logging your bird sightings in this powerful app. It will track your birding life list and will allow you to upload your images and audio recordings from your birding activities. It pairs nicely with the Merlin Bird ID app. Ebird.org
- Merlin Bird ID (Cornell Lab of Ornithology)—Highly recommended for beginners, this free app helps identify birds by answering a few questions or by recording the birds you hear. The app also provides photos and sounds for each species. Once you identify your bird, log your sighting in the eBird App. Merlin.allaboutbirds.org

ONLINE RESOURCES

- All About Birds (Cornell Lab of Ornithology)—Nationally respected resource for bird ID, sounds, and behavior, also referenced by local Audubon chapter.
- BirdWeb (Seattle Audubon/Birds Connect Seattle)—The definitive online guide to birds of Washington, with species accounts, photos, sounds, and site recommendations.
- Washington Ornithological Society (WOS) Birding Resources—Offers checklists, site guides, and a statewide birding community.

ORGANIZATIONS

- Birds Connect Seattle—Most regional areas—cities, counties, etc.—have birding organizations. Birds Connect Seattle (formerly Seattle Audubon) is one such group.
- Seattle Feminist Bird Club—There are lots of affinity-based birding groups. The Seattle Feminist Bird Club is one such group.
- Washington Audubon—Every state has an Audubon society, though some are changing their names given John James Audubon's challenging racist legacy.

LISTENING TO BIRDS

While most online birding guides have audio together with the images of birds, these resources are specifically aimed at sound.

- BirdNote—Seattle-based daily podcast sharing bird stories and conservation tips.
- Bird Song Basics: Getting started with Birding by Ear https://academy.allaboutbirds.org/product/bird-song-basics-getting-started-with-birding-by-ear/ This is a great, self-paced online class from Cornell Lab's Bird Academy. It will teach you how to listen to birds and identify them from their song.
- Cornell Lab's Macaulay Library—an excellent resource for bird song.

BIRD INDEX

Nycticorax nycticorax 36

O
Olive-sided Flycatcher 148
Osprey 62

P
Pandion haliaetus 62
Passer domesticus 210
Passerina amoena 242
Pelecanus erythrorhynchos 32
Pelecanus occidentalis californicus 34
Peregrine Falcon 150
Phalacrocorax auritus 42
Pica hudsonia 162
Pigeon guillemot 102
Pileated Woodpecker 152
Pine Siskin 212
Pipilo maculatus 248
Piranga ludoviciana 250
Poecile atricapillus 182
Pooecetes gramineus 218
Porzana carolina 68
Psaltriparus minimus 186
Purple finch 214

R
Red-breasted Nuthatch 190
Red-tailed Hawk 64
Red-winged Blackbird 216
Regulus calendula 192
Rhinoceros Auklet 104
Ring-necked Duck 20
Rock Pigeon 122
Ruby-crowned Kinglet 192

S
Sagebrush Sparrow 244
Sanderling 88
Sandhill Crane 66

W

Y

Z

PERMISSIONS AND PUBLICATION CREDITS

The editor and publisher gratefully acknowledge the permissions granted to reproduce the copyrighted material in this collection of prose and poems. Every effort has been made to trace copyright holders and obtain their permission. The publisher apologizes for any errors or omissions in the following list and would like to be notified of any corrections for future editions.

Carrie Albert, an earlier version of "They Met on a Telephone Line" was first published in the UK-based webzine *Ink Sweat & Tears*. The handmade poem-book version was added in 2021 to the same publication page. Reprinted by permission of the author.

Rae Armantrout, "Traveling" was published in *Go Figure* (Wesleyan University Press, 2024). Reprinted by permission of the author.

Subhaga Crystal Bacon, "Guillemot: Will, Desire, and Strength" was previously published in *humana obscura* (2022). Reprinted by permission of the author.

Linda Bierds, "The Swifts" originally appeared in *New England Review* (Vol. 31, No. 1, 2010), and was included in her book *Roget's Illusion* (G. P. Putnam's Sons, 2014). Reprinted by permission of the author.

Elizabeth Bradfield, "Kiss Me Like a Shoveler" was previously published in *SOFAR: Poems* (Persea Books, 2025). Reprinted by permission of the author.

Seattle Children's, "All About Me, The Greater Yellowlegs" is a student collaboration by five youths at Seattle Children's (formerly Seattle Children's Hospital).

Kevin Craft, "Margin of Error" appeared as "Wilson's Warbler" in *Vagrants & Accidentals* (University of Washington Press, 2017). Reprinted by permission of the author.

Constance Sidles, "Mother Ship" was originally published in *Forty-Six Views of Montlake Fill* (Constancy Press, 2014, artwork by Hiroko Seki). Reprinted by permission of the author.

Scot Siegel, "Pair of Greens" from *Tender Currencies* (MoonPath Press, 2025), winner of the Sally Albiso Book Award. Reprinted by permission of the author.

Martha Silano, "Hope is the Thing," was previously published in *Notre Dame Review* Summer/Fall 2021: New Life (Issue #52). Reprinted by permission of the author.

David Wagoner, "The Words," from *Traveling Light: Collected and New Poems*, copyright 1999 by David Wagoner. Used with permission of the University of Illinois Press.

Maya Jewell Zeller, "little spell for kestrel hovering/for x-ray & mothering," was previously published in *Underblong*, an online poetry journal, and *Alchemy for Cells & Other Beasts* (Entre Rios Books, 2017). Reprinted by permission of the author.

BIOGRAPHICAL NOTES: AUTHORS

MATEO ACUÑA-BRACKEN is a poet, librettist, and actor, who splits his time between Auburn and Seattle, Washington. He was the 2023–24 Seattle Youth Poet Laureate and currently serves as the 2024–26 Auburn Poet Laureate. As a librettist in the Seattle Opera Creation Lab, he developed the twenty-minute chamber opera *Blood Dawn of the Inti Sun* in collaboration with composer Mina Pariseau, which has since been performed around Puget Sound. His first chapbook, *Dear Spanish*, was published through Poetry NW Editions (2024). Mateo explores the languages of identity, heritage, and belonging.

KELLI RUSSELL AGODON is a bi/queer poet from Washington State whose next book, *Accidental Devotions*, will be published by Copper Canyon Press in 2026. Her previous collection, *Dialogues with Rising Tides*, was a finalist for the Washington State Book Awards. Kelli is the cofounder of Two Sylvias Press and teaches in Pacific Lutheran University's MFA program, the Rainier Writing Workshop. She is also the cohost of the poetry series "Poems You Need" with Melissa Studdard. Her favorite bird is the kingfisher. www.agodon.com / www.twosylviaspress.com / www.youtube.com/@PoemsYouNeed

CARRIE ALBERT creates to find healing and beauty in both words and visual art, often together. Her works are widely published. Recently, poems have appeared in *Anti-Heroin Chic*, *Gyroscope Review*, and *The Ekphrastic Review*; sculptures were included in exhibitions at Ghost Gallery and Bryn Mawr Hospital. She lives in Seattle with her papier-mâché animals.

Describing the poems in RAE ARMANTROUT's latest book, *Go Figure*, the *Library Journal* says, "she has honed enduring art on the ephemera that constitute a consciousness in motion through the present." Charles Bernstein says, "Her sheer, often hilarious, ingenuity is an aesthetic triumph." Armantrout's 2018 book, *Wobble*, was a finalist for the National Book Award that year. In 2010, *Versed* won the Pulitzer Prize for Poetry and The National Book Critics Circle Award. Her poems have appeared in many anthologies and journals, including *Poetry*,

Conjunctions, Lana Turner, The Nation, The New Yorker, The London Review of Books, Harpers, The Paris Review, Postmodern American Poetry: a Norton Anthology, and several editions of *The Best American Poetry*.

Former Washington State Poet Laureate **ELIZABETH AUSTEN** is the author of *Every Dress a Decision* (Blue Begonia Press), and the chapbooks *The Girl Who Goes Alone* and *Where Currents Meet*. She's performed her work in venues ranging from UNESCO in Paris to Holden Village in central Washington State. Her poems are featured in *Cascadia: Field Guide: Art, Ecology, Poetry, the New England Review*, and *Spirited Stone: Lessons from Kubota's Garden*, among other journals and anthologies. Elizabeth interviewed poets for NPR-affiliate KUOW radio for nearly twenty years, and now leads workshops in poetry and reflective writing for staff at Seattle Children's Hospital and other Pacific Northwest healthcare organizations.

DEBORAH BACHARACH is the author of two full-length poetry collections, *Shake & Tremor* (Grayson Books, 2021), and *After I Stop Lying* (Cherry Grove Collections, 2015). Her poems, book reviews, and essays have been published in *One Art, New Letters, Poet Lore,* and *The Writer's Chronicle*, among other journals. She has received numerous Pushcart Prize and Orison Prize nominations, and a Pushcart Prize honorable mention. She is currently a poetry reader for *SWWIM* and *Whale Road Review*. Find out more about her at DeborahBacharach.com.

SUBHAGA CRYSTAL BACON (they/them) is the author of five collections of poetry including *A Brief History of My Sex Life*, forthcoming from Lily Poetry Review Books; the Lambda Literary finalist, *Transitory* (2023), winner of the BOA Editions, Ltd. Isabella Gardner Award for Poetry; *Surrender of Water in Hidden Places*, winner of the Red Flag Poetry Chapbook Prize (2023), released in an expanded second edition in the summer of 2024. A Pushcart and Best of the Net nominee, Subhaga is a teaching artist working in schools and libraries with youth and adults, as well as private students. Their work appears in a variety of print and online journals. A Queer elder, they live in rural north central Washington on unceded Methow land.

CATHERINE BARNETT is the author of four poetry collections, including *Solutions for the Problem of Bodies in Space* (selected by Publishers Weekly as a "Best Books 2024" and included in NPR's "2024: Books We Love"); *Human Hours* (Believer Book Award, *New York Times* "Best Poetry of 2018" selection); *The Game of Boxes* (James Laughlin Award); and *Into Perfect Spheres Such Holes Are Pierced* (Beatrice Hawley Award). A Guggenheim and Civitella Ranieri fellow, she received a 2022 Arts and Letters Award in Literature from the American Academy of Arts and Letters, and a Whiting Award, among other recognitions. Her work has been published in the *The New Yorker, The NY Review of Books, The Yale Review, The Nation, Harper's, American Poetry Review,* and she has been included in *The Best American Poetry* three times. She teaches in NYU's MFA Program in Creative Writing and works as an independent editor.

ELLEN BASS's most recent book is *Indigo* (Copper Canyon Press, 2020). Her awards include Fellowships from the Guggenheim Foundation, NEA, Lambda Literary Award, and four Pushcart Prizes. She co-edited the first major anthology of women's poetry, *No More Masks!* (Doubleday, 1973), and she co-authored the groundbreaking *The Courage to Heal: A Guide for Women Survivors of Child Sexual Abuse* (Harper & Row, 1988). Chancellor Emerita of the Academy of American Poets, Bass founded poetry workshops at Salinas Valley State Prison and the Santa Cruz jails. She teaches in Pacific University's MFA program, and offers online Living Room Craft Talks at ellenbass.com.

LINDA BIERDS is the author of ten books of poetry. Her work has appeared in numerous publications, including *The Atlantic, The New Yorker, The Smithsonian, Poetry,* and *The Best American Poetry*. In addition to being awarded a MacArthur Foundation fellowship, Bierds has received support from the Ingram Merrill Foundation, the Guggenheim Memorial Foundation, the Rockefeller Foundation, and twice from the National Endowment for the Arts (NEA). She has served as a judge for some of the nation's most distinguished poetry prizes, including the Ruth Lilly Poetry Award, the Walt Whitman Poetry Award, and the National Book Award. She teaches the graduate poetry workshop at the University of Washington in Seattle.

DANI BLACKMAN's short prose has most recently appeared in *Bellingham Review, Fractured Lit, Citron Review, Epiphany, Witness,* and elsewhere. She was a finalist for the Reynolds Price Short Fiction award and a semifinalist for *The Best Small Fictions Anthology.* She teaches at North Seattle College. www.daniblackman.com.

MICHELE BOMBARDIER is the author of *What We Do,* a Washington State Book Award finalist, and the 2024 winner of the NORward Prize. Recent poems can be found in *New Ohio Review, JAMA, Atlanta Review, Parabola, Alaska Quarterly Review, Bellevue Literary Review,* and others. Her work has been read on NPR and set to music performed at OPERA America in NYC. She holds an MFA in poetry from Pacific University and has received support from Hedgebrook, Mineral School, The Tyrone Guthrie Centre, Edith Wharton House, and Humanities Washington. Michele is the founder of Fishplate Poetry, offering workshops to raise money for humanitarian aid; she is the inaugural Poet Laureate of Bainbridge Island, Washington.

ALLEN BRADEN is the author of *A Wreath of Down and Drops of Blood* (University of Georgia Press, 2010) and *Elegy in the Passive Voice.* His poems have been anthologized in *The Bedford Introduction to Literature, Poetry: An Introduction, Thinking and Writing about Poetry, Best New Poets, Spreading the Word: Editors on Poetry, Cascadia Field Guide, Dear Human at the Edge of Time: Poems on Climate Change in the United States, Attached to the Living World: A New Ecopoetry Anthology,* and *The World Is Charged: Poetic Engagements with Gerard Manley Hopkins.* He lives near the historic site of Fort Steilacoom in Lakewood, Washington.

ELIZABETH BRADFIELD's seven books include *SOFAR: Poems,* which includes poems that were published in *The Atlantic*

Monthly, The Sun, and *Orion; Interpretive Work,* which won
the Audre Lorde Prize in Lesbian Poetry; *Toward Antarctica;*
and the co-created *Cascadia Field Guide: Art, Ecology, Poetry,*
winner of a Pacific Northwest Book Award and a ForeWord
Indies Gold Medal. Editor-in-chief of *Broadsided* and a former
Wallace Stegner Fellow, Liz directs the Poetry Concentration
in the Western Colorado Low-residency MFA Program, teaches
at Brandeis University, and works as a naturalist and field
assistant on Cape Cod.

RONDA PISZK BROATCH is the author of *Chaos Theory for
Beginners* (MoonPath Press, 2023), finalist for the Sally Albiso
Prize, and *Lake of Fallen Constellations* (MoonPath Press, 2015).
Winner of the Willow Springs Surrealist Poetry Prize, Ronda's
journal publications include *Greensboro Review, Blackbird,
Sycamore Review, Missouri Review, Palette Poetry, Moon City
Review,* and NPR News / KUOW's *All Things Considered.* She is a
graduate student working toward her MFA at Pacific Lutheran
University's Rainier Writing Workshop. She is a cat-herder
with a fascination for quantum physics, astrophysics, the lives
of poets, and other sorts of chaos. Ronda communes with
ravens and barred owls, and lives on Port Gamble S'Klallam
Tribal land.

SHARON M. CARTER is a poet and visual artist, originally from
Lancashire, England, who lives on the Olympic Peninsula in
the Pacific Northwest. She recently retired from a career in
healthcare. She is indebted to the Hedgebrook Foundation
and the Jack Straw Writers Program for their support during
her writing process. Her work has been published in many
journals, including the *Amsterdam Quarterly, Terra Nova, The
Madrona Project, Ars Medica, Quartet* and *One Art.* Her poetry
book, *Quiver,* was published in 2022. *Ekphrastic Pastiche,* a
compilation of poetry and original drawings, was published in
2024. www.sharonmcarter.com

KEVIN CRAFT lives in Seattle and directs the Written Arts
Program at Everett Community College. For two decades
he also served as a faculty director of the University of
Washington's Writers in Rome Program. His books include

Traverse (Lynx House Press, 2024), *Vagrants & Accidentals* (University of Washington Press, 2017), and *Solar Prominence* (Cloudbank Books, 2005). Favorite writing / birding gigs include Writer in Residence at Olympic National Park and volunteer lookout in the North Cascades. Editor of *Poetry Northwest* from 2009–2016, he is currently Executive Editor of Poetry NW Editions.

LAURA DA' is a poet and teacher who studied at the Institute of American Indian Arts. She is the author of *Tributaries*, an American Book Award winner, *Instruments of the True Measure*, Washington State Book Award winner, and *Severalty*, forthcoming in 2025. Da' is Eastern Shawnee, and she lives in Washington State with her family.

MICHAEL DALEY's eighth poetry collection, *Ground Work*, is forthcoming from Ravenna Press. He is the founder and former publisher of Empty Bowl Press, as well as the editor of *The Madrona Project*, an anthology series.

KRISTIE FREDERICK DAUGHERTY is a poet and professor. She holds an MFA in Poetry from Vermont College of Fine Arts. She is also a PhD candidate in Literature/Criticism at the Indiana University of Pennsylvania. She is the editor of *Invisible Strings: 113 Poets Respond to the Songs of Taylor Swift*, which was published in December 2024 from Random House. Her poems have been featured in *Ponder Review, North American Review, American Poetry Review,* and various other literary journals. Her collection of poems, *Ordinary Pietá*, is forthcoming in 2026.

C. HUNTER DAVIS, a poet who lives among birds, writes a column on birds, and sometimes wishes she was a bird. Currently, she has three published books: *The A Poems, Beauty,* and *This is Enough.*

OLIVER DE LA PAZ is the author and editor of several books, and serves as the Poet Laureate of Worcester, Massachusetts. His latest collection of poetry, *The Diaspora Sonnets*, was published by Liveright Press (2023). It was a winner of the

2023 New England Book Award and was longlisted for the 2023 National Book Award. A founding member of Kundiman, he teaches at the College of the Holy Cross (Worcester, Massachusetts)and in the Low-Residency MFA Program at Pacific Lutheran University.

RISA DENENBERG lives on the Olympic Peninsula in Washington State, where she works as a nurse practitioner and volunteers with End-of-Life Washington. She is a co-founder of Headmistress Press, publisher of books of poems by Lesbians, and the curator of the online *The Poetry Cafe*, a site where poetry chapbooks are celebrated and reviewed. She has published eight collections of poetry, most recently *Rain/ Dweller* (MoonPath Press, 2024). She is currently working on a memoir titled *Mother, Interrupted*.

PAMELA MOORE DIONNE is a frequent birder and a Port Townsend, Washington poet / writer / visual artist. She's married to Ron and owned by a Vizsla dog named Magda, for whom she is tasked with long pleasant walks through forests. She is the author of two chapbooks, *Paradox and Illusion*, and *Taut Caesuras*, both from Finishing Line Press. Dionne earned her MFA from Goddard College. Her website can be found at www.pamelamooredionne.com.

RACHEL EDELMAN, author of *Dear Memphis* (River River Books, 2024), is a Jewish poet who writes into diasporic living. Their poems, essays, and epistles have been published in *West Branch, Lilith, Orion, AGNI,* and many other journals. They teach Language Arts in the Seattle Public Schools, where embodiment and care root their personal, poetic, and pedagogical practice.

KATY E. ELLIS' second book of poetry, *Forty Bouts in the Wilderness*, was first runner-up for the 2024 MoonPath Press Sally Albiso Award. She is also the author of the novel-length prose poem *Home Water, Home Land* (Tolsun Books), and three chapbooks, including the award-winning *Night Watch* (Floating Bridge Press), *Urban Animal Expeditions* (Dancing Girl Press), and *Gravity* (Yellow Flag Press)—a single poem which was nominated for a Pushcart Prize. Her work has appeared in a number of literary journals and anthologies including *Mom Egg Review, SWWIM, Pithead Chapel, Rise Up, Literary Mama, MAYDAY Magazine, Burnside Review,* and in the Canadian journals *PRISM International, Grain* and *Fiddlehead.* Learn more at www.KatyEEllis.com

BEVERLY FESHARAKI's poems have appeared in numerous journals, including *Bangalore Review, Typishly, Moria, 3Elements Review, Indolent Books, Anti Heroin Chic,* and *So To Speak,* as well as on the website of the Museum of Northwest Art and in the anthology, *Women Writing: On The Edge of Dark and Light.* She was a long-time member of Inscape Poets in Tacoma, Washington, and she writes with Poets on the Coast in LaConner, Washington, every September. Bev lives with her husband in Mukilteo, Washington.

KATHLEEN FLENNIKEN's newest collection of poetry is *Dressing in the Dark* (Lynx House, 2025). She is the recipient of fellowships from the NEA and Artist Trust, a Pushcart Prize, and the *Prairie Schooner* Book Prize. Her previous books include *Post Romantic* (University of Washington Press, 2020), which was a finalist for the Washington State Book Award; *Plume* (University of Washington Press 2012), a finalist for the William Carlos Williams Award from the Poetry Society of America and winner of the Washington State Book Award; and *Famous* (University of Nebraska Press, 2006), named a Notable Book by the American Library Association. Her poems have appeared in *Willow Springs Review, Image,* and the *Poetry Unbound* and *Cascadia Field Guide* anthologies. She served as Washington State Poet Laureate from 2012–2014.

STACY D. FLOOD: Originally from Buffalo, and currently living in Seattle, Flood's work has been performed and published nationwide as well as across the Puget Sound Area. He has been a finalist in the Playwrights Foundation Bay Area, Ashland New Play, and ACT New Play Northwest festivals; and, in addition, he was an artist-in-residence at *DISQUIET* in Lisbon, *Djerassi* in Northern California, *Oberpfälzer Künstlerhaus* in Bavaria, and *Millay Arts* in New York. Furthermore, he is the recipient of a

Getty Fellowship to the *Community of Writers*, and his novella, entitled *The Salt Fields*, is an editor's choice pick for both *Shelf Awareness* and the Historical Novel Society.

CAROLYN FORCHÉ is the author of five books of poetry, most recently *In the Lateness of the World* (Penguin Press, 2020), a finalist for the Pulitzer Prize; *Blue Hour* (2004), a finalist for the National Book Critics Circle Award; *The Angel of History* (1995), winner of the Los Angeles Times Book Award; *The Country Between Us* (1982), winner of the Lamont Prize of the Academy of American Poets; and *Gathering the Tribes* (1976), winner of the Yale Series of Younger Poets Prize. She is the author of the prose book, *What You Have Heard Is True: A Memoir of Witness and Resistance* (Penguin Press, 2019), winner of the Juan E. Méndez Book Award for Human Rights in Latin America and a finalist for the National Book Award. Her anthology, *Against Forgetting*, has been praised by Nelson Mandela as "itself a blow against tyranny, against prejudice, against injustice." She lives in Maryland with her husband, photographer Harry Mattison.

LEA GALANTER is a professional copy editor with a BA in History, post-graduate work in Journalism, and an MA in Early Celtic Studies. After writing plays and being involved in the Seattle theater community for many years, she stumbled into the world of poetry and has never looked back. Her poems have been published by *Chiron Review, River & South Review, Panoply, Young Raven's Literary Review, Poetica Review, Unlost Journal,* and *Red Coyote,* as well as in several anthologies. She owns Gallant Editorial Services and loves to help authors make their manuscripts shine. After more than thirty years in the Pacific Northwest, she now calls Massachusetts home. She is also a student of metaphysics and will gladly pull cards for friends and family.

ROBBIE GAMBLE (he/him) received an MFA in Poetry from Lesley University. His poems and essays have appeared in *DIALOGIST, Post Road, Pangyrus, Salamander, The Sun,* and *Tahoma Literary Review.* His chapbook, *A Can of Pinto Beans,* published by Lily Poetry Review Press, was a finalist for the 2022 Jean

Pedrick Award. Robbie was the winner of the 2017 Carve Poetry Prize, and he was a 2019 Robert Taylor fellow at the Kenyon Summer Writers Workshop. His essay "Exit Wound" was cited as a notable essay in *The Best American Essays 2020*. Robbie is the poetry editor for *Solstice Literary Magazine,* and he divides his time between Boston and Vermont.

MATT GANO is author of *Suits for the Swarm,* and a recording artist releasing music under the title, Entendres. Matt's work in performance, on the page, and in the classroom, spans two decades in the Pacific Northwest and has led to invitations as a guest instructor at the Juilliard School in NYC, resident guest artist and instructor at the Lee Shau Kee School of Creativity in Hong Kong, and repeat panelist and featured poet for the Skagit River Poetry Festival (2013-2024). Matt works for the Greater Seattle Bureau of Fearless Ideas, and is co-founder of the Seattle Youth Poet Laureate program.

JENNY GEORGE is the author of *After Image* (2024) and *The Dream of Reason* (2018), both from Copper Canyon Press. She is also a winner of the *Boston Review's* Unterberg Discovery Poetry Contest (2015), and a recipient of fellowships from the Bread Loaf Writers' Conference, Lannan Foundation, MacDowell, and Yaddo. Her poems have appeared in *The New York Times, Poetry, Ploughshares, Kenyon Review, Narrative, Granta, Iowa Review, Orion, Los Angeles Review of Books, Poem-A-Day* at *Poets.org,* and elsewhere. Jenny lives in Santa Fe, New Mexico, where she works in social justice philanthropy.

ALLISON GREEN is the author of a novel, *Half-Moon Scar* (St. Martin's Press, 2000), a memoir, *The Ghosts Who Travel with Me: A Literary Pilgrimage Through Brautigan's America* (Ooligan Press, 2015), and essays that have appeared in publications such as *The Rumpus, The Common,* and *Calyx.* Her essay, "Twenty Hours and Ten Minutes of Therapy," was published in *The Gettysburg Review,* reprinted in *Utne Reader,* and listed as a Notable Essay in *The Best American Essays.*

JACQUELINE HASKINS, an aquatic ecologist writing from her self-built strawbale home, loves plunging into ice-cold mountain streams, cypress swamps, indie bookstores, and craft beers. Her forthcoming poetry collection, *River Kith* (Fernwood Press, 2026), was honored as a Homebound finalist. Her wellness memoir, *Kickass Healthy LADA* (Hachette, 2023), received a Silver Nautilus, won the American BookFest Award in Health, was a Feathered Quill Finalist, and a five-star Reader's Favorite. Other recognition for her poetry and essays includes *Oregon Quarterly's* Northwest Perspectives finalist, *Glimmer Train* finalist, Pushcart nominee, and *Soundings Review* Award. Jacqueline's work appears in *Terrain, The Iowa Review, River Teeth, Cirque Journal, Raven Chronicles,* and many other journals.

LYANDA LYNN HAUPT is an award-winning author, naturalist, ecophilosopher, and speaker whose work explores the beautiful, complicated connections between humans and the wild, natural world. She is a winner of the Sigurd Olson Nature Writing Award, the Nautilus Book Award Grand Prize, and is a two-time winner of the Washington State Book Award. Her newest book is *Rooted: Life at the Crossroads of Science, Nature, and Spirit* (Little, Brown Spark, 2021, 2023). She lives in the mossy green woods of the Pacific Northwest, where she writes, spins wool, communes with owls, and knits magical hats.

KATELYNN HIBBARD's books are *Sleeping Upside Down* (Silverfish Review Press, 2006, winner of the Gerald Cable Book Award), *Sweet Weight* (Tiger Bark Press, 2012), *Simples*, winner of the 2018 Howling Bird Press Poetry Prize, and *Unblossoming* (Tiger Bark Press, 2025). She earned an MFA at the University of Oregon, while enjoying the local flora and fauna and studying with Dorianne Laux, Garrett Hongo, and T.R. Hummer. Her work has appeared in numerous print and online venues, including *Plant-Human Quarterly, Notre Dame Review,* and *Prairie Schooner.* Editor of *When We Become Weavers: Queer Female Poets on the Midwest Experience* (Squares & Rebels Press, 2012), she lives with her spouse Jan and many pets in Saint Paul, Minnesota. Please visit katelynnhibbard.com for more information.

JANE HIRSHFIELD: Writing "some of the most important poetry in the world today" (*The New York Times Magazine*), Hirshfield is the author of ten poetry collections, most recently *The Asking: New & Selected Poems* (Knopf, 2023); two collections of essays; and four books collecting and co-translating world poets from the deep past. Hirshfield's honors include the Poetry Center Book Award, the California Book Award, and finalist selection for the National Book Critics Circle Award. Her work has been translated into eighteen languages, Hirshfield is a former chancellor of the Academy of American Poets, founder of Poets for Science, and an elected member of the American Academy of Arts & Sciences.

PAUL HLAVA CEBALLOS is the author of *banana [ ]*, winner of the AWP Donald Hall Prize for Poetry and the Poetry Society of America's Norma Farber First Book Award; also a finalist for the National Book Critics Circle Award and the Kate Tufts Discovery Award. His collaborative chapbook, *Banana [ ] / we pilot the blood,* shares pages with Quenton Baker and Christina Sharpe. He is a CantoMundo fellow and has been featured on *The Poetry Magazine* Podcast and Seattle's *The Stranger.* He currently is the Poetry Editor of the *Seattle Met Magazine,* and practices echocardiography.

REBECCA HOOGS is the author of *Self-Storage* (Stephen F. Austin State University Press), which was a finalist for the 2013 Washington State Book Award in Poetry, and a chapbook, *Grenade* (GreenTower Press, 2005). Her poems have appeared in *Poetry, AGNI, FIELD, Crazyhorse, Cascadia Field Guide, Zyzzyva, Poetry Northwest,* and others. She is the Executive Director of Seattle Arts & Lectures.

DIDI L. JACKSON is the author of the poetry collections *My Infinity* (2024) and *Moon Jar* (2020). Her poems have appeared in *American Poetry Review, Bomb, The New Yorker,* and *World Literature Today,* among other journals and magazines. She has had poems selected for *The Best American Poetry,* the Academy of American Poets' *Poem-a-day,* and *The Slowdown* podcast with Tracy K. Smith. She is the recipient of the Robert H. Winner Memorial Award from the Poetry Society of America. She is a Dean's Faculty Fellow at Vanderbilt University in Nashville, Tennessee, where she teaches creative writing. Most recently she completed her certification as a Tennessee Naturalist.

MAJOR JACKSON is the author of *Razzle Dazzle: New & Selected Poems 2002–2022*. He is the inaugural recipient of the Patricia Cannon Willis Prize for American Poetry, and an Academy of American Poets Fellowship. He is the Gertrude Vanderbilt Chair in the Humanities at Vanderbilt University. Website: www.majorjackson.com.

LOWELL JONS is an adventurer at heart, whether as an elementary school teacher (yikes), biking in Antarctica, getting sniffed by a wolf, kayaking over whales, staring nose to nose with a bear . . . you get the picture. His poetry has been published in Northwest publications, discussed in a podcast, and as public art—as well as had an essay published in a national publication. His photography is in private collections, business advertising, as well in national publications. He has lived in the Salish Sea region for forty-two years, and is now living in the San Juan Islands.

ANYA KIRSHBAUM is a bi/queer poet, a somatic therapist, and a later-in-life mama from Seattle, Washington. Her work has appeared in *Whale Road Review, Sweet Lit, SWWIM, MER-Mom Egg Review, Crannóg, Solstice Literary Magazine,* and elsewhere. She was a finalist for the New Millennium Writing Awards and the Patricia Dobler Poetry Award; she was nominated for the 2024 Forward Prize for Best Single Poem, and was the recipient of the 2023 Banyan Poetry Prize. She is currently at work on her first collection.

TED KOOSER is a former United States Poet Laureate (2004-2006), and winner of the Pulitzer Prize for Poetry (*Delights and Shadows*, Copper Canyon Press, 2004). He is a retired life insurance executive and Presidential Professor of English at the University of Nebraska. His most recent collection of poems is *Raft* (Copper Canyon Press, 2024).

SUSAN LANDGRAF's *Out of a Land of Alkali and Chromate* was published by Moonpath Press in 2025. An Academy of

American Poet Laureates Fellowship resulted in *A Muckleshoot Poetry Anthology: From the Confluence of the Green and White Rivers* (WSU Press, 2024). Other books include *Journey of Trees* (2024), *Crossings, The Inspired Poet, What We Bury Changes the Ground,* and *Other Voices.* More than 400 poems have appeared in *Nimrod, Prairie Schooner, Poet Lore,* and others. Landgraf's given more than 150 workshops in the U.S. and abroad. A former journalist, she taught thirty years at Highline College, and at Shanghai Jiao Tong University four different times. She was Auburn Poet Laureate from 2018-2020. Alphabetically speaking, she loves birds, books, epiphanies, family, friends, octopuses, oysters, and travel.

ROBERT LASHLEY was a 2016 Jack Straw Fellow, Artist Trust Fellow, and a nominee for a Stranger Genius Award. His books include *Green River Valley* (Blue Cactus Press, 2021), *Up South* (Small Doggies Press, 2017), and *The Homeboy Songs* (Small Doggies Press, 2014). His poetry has appeared in *The Seattle Review of Books, Poetry Northwest, McSweeneys,* and the anthologies *The Cascadia Field Guide* and *Cascadian Zen.* In 2019, *Entropy Magazine* named *The Homeboy Songs* one of the twenty-five essential books to come out of Seattle. His novel, *I Never Dreamed You'd Leave In Summer,* was selected as a finalist for a 2024 Washington State Book Award in Fiction (Demersal Publishing, 2024), and in 2025, the novel was selected as one of bookshop.com's thirty favorite Black books in the last ten years. He lives in Bellingham, Washington.

CLAUDIA CASTRO LUNA is an Academy of American Poets Laureate Fellow (2019), Washington State Poet Laureate (2018–2021), and Seattle's inaugural Civic Poet (2015-2018). She is the author of *Cipota Under the Moon* (Tia Chucha Press, 2022) and *Killing Marías* (Two Sylvias Press, 2017), both shortlisted for the Washington State Book Award in Poetry—2023 and 2018 respectively. She is also the author of *One River, A Thousand Voices* (Chin Music Press, 2020), and the chapbook *This City* (Floating Bridge Press, 2016). Her most recent non-fiction is in *There's a Revolution Outside, My Love: Letters from a Crisis* (Vintage, 2021) and in *Memory's Vault: The Poetic Heart of Fort Worden* (Empty Bowl Press,). Born in El Salvador, Castro Luna lives in English and Spanish, and she writes and teaches in Seattle on unceded Duwamish lands.

ANNE HAVEN MCDONNELL lives in Santa Fe, New Mexico, where she teaches as a full professor of Creative Writing at the Institute of American Indian Arts. A recipient of fellowships from the National Endowment of the Arts (2023) and MacDowell, she is the author of *Breath on a Coal* (Middle Creek Press, 2022), and the chapbook *Living with Wolves* (Split Rock Press, 2020). Her forthcoming book of poems is *Singing Under Snow,* winner of the Wheelbarrow Books Prize at MSU Press. Her poetry has been published in *Orion Magazine, Academy of American Poets Poem-a-Day, The Georgia Review, Narrative Magazine, Nimrod Journal, Terrain.org,* and elsewhere. Anne Haven is a poetry editor for the online journal *Terrain.org.*

KRISTIE MCLEAN is a storyteller and social activist whose work has appeared on National Public Radio's *All Things Considered,* and in the *Huffington Post, The Circle Way, Developing Women's Leadership Around the Globe, Hamlin Fistula and Salaam Garage: Stories of Ethiopia from 12 Citizen Journalists; Women of the World: Afghanistan and Guinea Bissau; the King County Journal, Chicken Soup For the Traveler's Soul, The Bellingham Review, Leader, Blue, Jeopardy,* and *Pontoon* magazines, Audubon Society, and the United Methodist Publishing House. She has worked and traveled in more than fifty countries on six continents, and her photography has been showcased in Washington State and at global summits in Europe and Asia. Kristie serves as Executive Director for Communities of Belonging, a non-profit that supports those moving beyond incarceration and homelessness. She lives in West Seattle and enjoys polar plunges in Puget Sound and snuggling with her tuxedo cat, Ollie.

ERIN MALONE is the author of *Site of Disappearance* (Ornithopter, 2023), *Hover* (Tebot Bach, 2015), and a chapbook, *What Sound Does It Make* (Concrete Wolf, 2008). She has received grants and fellowships from Washington State Artist Trust, 4Culture, Jack Straw, and the Colorado Council of the Arts; and residency support from Kimmel-

Harding Nelson Center, The Anderson Center, Ucross, Jentel, and Monson Arts. Her poems have appeared in journals such as *FIELD, New Ohio Review, North American Review, Cimarron,* and *Beloit Poetry Journal.* Formerly Editor of *Poetry Northwest*, Erin taught at the University of Colorado at Colorado Springs, the University of Washington, Hugo House, and with Seattle's Writers in the Schools. She lives on Bainbridge Island, Washington.

JAYNE MAREK (October 16, 1954–January 9, 2025) earned a PhD from the University of Wisconsin-Madison and an MFA from the University of Notre Dame. Nominated for Best of the Net and Pushcart Prizes, she won the *Last Stanza Poetry Journal* Editor's Choice Award and the Bill Holm Witness Poetry Prize. She held residencies at Playa, the Whiteley Center, and Hypatia-in-the-Woods. Her full-length poetry collections included *Torrential* (2025), *Dusk-Voiced* (2024), *The Tree Surgeon Dreams of Bowling* (2018), and *In and Out of Rough Water* (2017). Scholarly work included *Women Editing Modernism: "Little" Magazines and Literary History* (1995) and the *Index to Poetry Magazine* covering the years 1912-1997. She made her home in the Pacific Northwest near the wild and beautiful coast, prior to passing away in January 2025.

JENNIFER MARKELL's first poetry collection, *Samsara* (Turning Point, 2014), was named a "Must Read" by the Massachusetts Book Awards. Her second collection, *Singing at High Altitude,* was published in 2021 by The Main Street Rag. She has received awards from the Chester H. Jones Foundation, *The Comstock Review,* The New England Poetry Club, and the Rita Dove Prize for women writers at Salem College. Many birds have landed in Jennifer's poems. Her work has appeared or is forthcoming in numerous journals, including *The Bitter Oleander, Cutthroat, Diode, The MacGuffin, RHINO, Storm Cellar,* and *The Women's Review of Books.* In her work as a psychotherapist and writer, she believes in the power of words to help us feel what we feel and know what we know.

JENNIFER MARTELLI has received fellowships from The Virginia Center for the Creative Arts, Monson Arts, and the

Massachusetts Cultural Council. Her work has appeared in The Academy of American Poets *Poem-A-Day, Poetry, Best of the Net Anthology, Braving the Body Anthology, Verse Daily, Plume, The Tahoma Literary Review, Diode,* and elsewhere. She is the author of *Psychic Party Under the Bottle Tree, The Queen of Queens*—which won the Italian American Studies Association Book Award and was shortlisted for the Massachusetts Book Award—and *My Tarantella,* which was also shortlisted for the Massachusetts Book Award and named finalist for the Housatonic Book Award. Jennifer is co-poetry editor for *MER.* www.jennmartelli.com.

An award-winning poet and short story writer, GERALDINE MILLS is the author of six collections of poetry, three collections of short stories, and two children's novels. She is a regular visitor to Washington State to see her family and grandchildren and to meet up with her friend of many years, poet and editor Susan Rich. Her fiction and poetry have been on curricula of contemporary literature courses in a number of US universities, and the USA summer program at the Burren College of Art, Ireland. Her most recent poetry collection is *When the Light, New and Selected Poems,* published by Arlen House in 2023.

CHLOE MOHS is a twenty-two-year-old queer writer and poet born and raised in the Pacific Northwest. They've had poetry published in the *Voices of Tacoma: A Gathering of Poets* (anthology) and *The Diamond Gazette.* They also have multiple short stories featured in *Broken Antler Magazine.* Mohs is currently writing her first novel amongst a multitude of other projects, as she cannot be held down by one genre, though she is partial to speculative fiction and strange poetry. She can be found @chloe._.mohs on instagram.

JEANNE MOREL is the author of the chapbooks *I See My Way to Some Partial Results* (Ravenna Press), *Jackpot* (Bottlecap Press), and *That Crossing Is Not Automatic* (Tarpaulin Sky Press). Her poem, "Loss & Other Forms of Death," was selected by Leila Chatti for the 2021 Fugue Poetry Prize. She lives in Seattle and writes about other places.

MALENA MÖRLING is the author of two poetry books: *Ocean Avenue* and *Astoria*. Her third book of poetry is forthcoming from Alice James Books in 2026. She has published translations of work by Nobel Laureate Tomas Tranströmer and many other Swedish poets. She edited and translated *The Star by My Head,* an anthology of Swedish poets, with Jonas Ellerström. She has received a Lannan Literary Fellowship, a John Simon Guggenheim Fellowship, and a Dianna L. Bennett Fellowship from the Beverly Rogers, Carol C. Harter Black Mountain Institute. She is a Professor of Creative Writing at The University of North Carolina, Wilmington.

MULCH MORWELL is a Seattle local poet, bird photographer, and visual artist. In their work Mulch often focuses on things such as death, queerness, and what it means to be a human person relating to other human people in a world which often feels out of control. Mulch rediscovered a love of poetry working for Youth Speaks Seattle, and finds it to be a wonderful form of expression for both youth and adults. Mulch has always loved birds and would often try to catch geese as a child; they're still puzzled as to why the one time they caught one it didn't injure them and instead showed its dissatisfaction with the situation by peeing.

ERIN MURPHY is the author or editor of more than a dozen books, including *Human Resources* (2025), *Fluent in Blue* (2024), *Taxonomies* (2022), and *Fields of Ache* (2022)—a chapbook of centos that is available for a free download from Ghost City Press. Her work has appeared in *Ecotone, Women's Studies Quarterly, Rattle, The Best of Brevity,* and *Best Microfiction 2024,* and in anthologies from Random House, Bloomsbury, and Bedford/St. Martin's. Her awards include a Dorothy Sargent Rosenberg Poetry Prize, two Foreword INDIES Book of the Year Awards, the Paterson Prize for Literary Excellence, and a Best of the Net Award. She is professor of English at Penn State Altoona and poetry editor of *The Summerset Review*. Website: www.erin-murphy.com

ABBY E. MURRAY (they/them) is the editor of *Collateral*, a literary journal concerned with the impact of violent conflict and military service beyond the combat zone. Their first book, *Hail and Farewell: Poems* (2019), won the Perugia Press Poetry Prize and was a finalist for the Washington State Book Award. Their second book, *Recovery Commands*, recently won the Richard-Gabriel Rummonds Poetry Prize and will be published by Ex Ophidia Press in 2025. Abby served as the 2019-2021 Poet Laureate for the city of Tacoma, Washington, and currently teaches rhetoric in military strategy to Army War College fellows at the University of Washington.

ARLENE NAGANAWA's work appears in *Calyx, Fatal Flaw, La Piccioletta Barca, Mom Egg Review, The Inflectionist, Thimble, Waxwing, West Trestle Review, Whale Road Review* and other journals. Her collections include *I Weave a Nest of Foil* (Kelson Books), *We Were Talking about When We Had Bodies* (Ravenna Press), *The Ark and the Bear* (Floating Bridge Press), *The Scarecrow Bride* (Red Bird Chapbooks), and *Private Graveyard* (Gribble Press). Her poems were featured in 4Culture's Poetry on Buses/Poetry in Public: Places of Landing. She received grants from City Artist Seattle and Artist Trust. She was a Writer in the Schools for Seattle Arts and Lectures, a Hugo House youth instructor, and a Pongo poetry mentor with incarcerated youth.

GREG NOVEMBER is a short story writer, English instructor at North Seattle College and Highline College, and formerly a senior submissions reader for *New England Review*. In recent years, he's been the recipient of a fellowship from the Jack Straw Cultural Center, nominated for Best of the Net, and a finalist in fiction contests from Black Lawrence Press, *Fractured Lit, december,* and *The Missouri Review*. His work has most recently appeared in *Boulevard, Carve, The Raleigh Review, Hawaii Pacific Review, Epiphany,* and *Juked,* among other places. He has an MFA from UC, Irvine, and lives with his wife and two children in Seattle, Washington.

NAOMI SHIHAB NYE is an award-winning Palestinian-American poet, essayist, educator, and editor whose work has appeared widely. She edited the American Library Association (ALA) Notable international poetry collection *This Same Sky,* and

The Tree Is Older Than You Are: A Bilingual Gathering of Poems & Stories from Mexico, as well as *The Space Between Our Footsteps: Poems and Paintings from the Middle East.* Her books of poems include *Fuel, Red Suitcase, 19 Varieties of Gazelle: Poems of the Middle East* (a finalist for the National Book Award), and *Words Under the Words.* A Guggenheim fellow, she is also the author of the young adult novel *Habibi,* winner of the Jane Addams Children's Book Award. Naomi was honored to be a friend of recently departed and much beloved Victor Emanuel of Texas, one of the greatest friends of birds in the world. Naomi lives in San Antonio, Texas, with her husband Michael.

PETER PEREIRA is a family physician and poet in Seattle. His poems have appeared in *Poetry, Prairie Schooner, Virginia Quarterly Review,* and other magazines. They have also been featured on *The Writer's Almanac,* BBC Radio, and in *The Best American Poetry* anthology. His books include *Saying the World* and *What's Written on the Body,* both from Copper Canyon Press, and the limited edition chapbook, *The Lost Twin,* from Grey Spider Press.

LUCIA PERILLO (1958–2016) grew up in the suburbs of New York City in the 1960s. Perillo taught at Syracuse University, Southern Illinois University, Saint Martin's University, and in the Warren Wilson MFA program. Her work appeared in *The New Yorker, The Atlantic,* and *The Kenyon Review,* among other magazines. A traditional poet of mostly free-verse personal reflection, she wrote extensively about living with multiple sclerosis in her poems and essays. *Time Will Clean the Carcass Bones* was her last book of poetry (Copper Canyon Press, 2016). Her 2012 collection of short fiction, *Happiness is a Chemical in the Brain,* was shortlisted for the 2013 PEN/Robert W. Bingham Prize. Her other honors include the MacArthur Foundation "Genius" Grant in 2000, and the recognition of her *Inseminating the Elephant* (2009) as a finalist for the Pulitzer Prize.

LAURA URBAN PERRY is a poet, artist, and award-winning graphic designer. She earned a BFA from the University of Washington. Now she devotes her time to poetry, painting, and photography. Her work has been published in the *Amsterdam Quarterly, Poets on the Coast Anthologies* and *Telephone*—an international digital artists game. Laura lives in Seattle and sometimes in a cabin she built with her husband and kids on an island with no roads.

ABI POLLOKOFF is the author of *night myths · · before the body* (Red Hen Press, 2025). A Pushcart Prize nominee and recipient of the Anselle M. Larson / Academy of American Poets Prize, her poems can be found in *Triquarterly, The Seventh Wave, Denver Quarterly,* and *Radar,* where she was a finalist for the Coniston Prize. Abi has been supported by organizations such as the Jack Straw Cultural Center, Hugo House, and AWP, where she was a 2024 Writer to Writer Mentee. Abi is the managing editor for Poetry NW Editions and works in publishing. She received her MFA from the University of Washington. Find her at abipollokoff.com.

CYNTHIA R. PRATT is a founding member of the Olympia Poetry Network's board which has been in existence for thirty-five years. Her poems have appeared in numerous journals including *Raven Chronicles, The RavensPerch, The Writing Disorder, The Last Stanza Poetry Journal, Kestrel Journal, Third Wednesday Magazine,* and in six anthologies, including Washington Humanities and Empty Bowl Press's *I Sing the Salmon Home* (2023). She also has poems in three other upcoming anthologies. Her manuscript, *Celestial Drift,* was published in 2016. A former Lacey Councilmember and Deputy Mayor of the City of Lacey for the last twelve years, her term ended in December 2021. She is the first Poet Laureate of Lacey as of 2022. She reads too many murder mysteries and talks to birds. Website: Cynthia-pratt-poet.net.

RENA PRIEST is an enrolled member of the Lhaq'temish (Lummi) Nation and served as the sixth Washington State Poet Laureate (2021-2023). Priest is the recipient of a Washington State Book Award and has received fellowships from the Academy of American Poets, Indigenous Nations Poets, Nia Tero, and the University of Washington Libraries. Her first collection, *Patriarchy Blues,* won an American Book Award. Her second collection, *Sublime Subliminal,* was published as the finalist for the Floating Bridge Press Chapbook Award. She has published a non-fiction book, *Northwest Know-how: Beaches,* with Sasquatch Books, and is the editor of two anthologies: *I Sing the Salmon Home: Poems from Washington State* and *The Larger Voice: Celebrating Native Arts and Culture Foundation Literature Fellows.* Her forthcoming collection of essays, *Positively Uncivilized,* will be published in September 2025 by Raven Chronicles Press as the inaugural winner of their 2025 Keepers of the Fire Award. She lives in Bellingham, Washington.

Czech-American artist and American Book Award winner SHANN RAY teaches leadership and forgiveness studies at Gonzaga University and poetry at Stanford University. A National Endowment for the Arts Fellow, through his research in forgiveness and genocide Shann has served as a visiting scholar in Africa, Asia, Europe, and the Americas, and as a poetry mentor for the PEN America Prison and Justice Writers Program. He has collaborated as a visiting poet with painter Makoto Fujimura on a United Nations grant entitled *Intercultural Dialogues through Beauty as a Language of Peace.* Shann is a three-time High Plains Book Award winner, Bread Loaf Fellow, Bakeless Prize winner, and winner of the Foreword Book of the Year Readers' Choice Award. His poems and prose have been featured in *Poetry, Esquire, Narrative, McSweeney's, Prairie Schooner, Poetry International, Big Sky Journal,* and *The American Journal of Poetry.*

BETHANY REID's fourth full-length collection of poems, *The Pear Tree: Elegy for a Farm,* won the 2023 Sally Albiso Award from MoonPath Press. Her essays, book reviews, stories, and poems have recently appeared in or are forthcoming from *Raven Chronicles, Poetry East, Tendon, After Images,* and the online journal *Escape Into Life.* Bethany leads a weekly writing workshop, teaches poetry classes for the Creative Retirement Institute (CRI), and blogs about writing and life at http://www.bethanyareid.com.

SUSAN RICH: See Biographical Notes: Editorial Staff

ANDREW ROBIN is the author of the poetry collections *Something has to happen next,* which was awarded the Iowa Poetry Prize, *Good Beast,* a finalist for the Oregon Book Award, and *Stray Birds,* a finalist for the Washington State Book Award. Honors include a Poetry Society of America National Chapbook Fellowship and a Distinguished Teaching Award in English from the University of Massachusetts Amherst. An RN specializing in cardiac and urgent care, Andrew lives with his wife Sarah north of Seattle on *Sx'wálech* (Lopez Island) in the unceded ancestral waterways of the Coast Salish peoples.

DIANE SEUSS's sixth collection is *Modern Poetry* (Graywolf Press, 2024), a finalist for the National Book Award. *frank: sonnets* (Graywolf Press, 2021) was the winner of the National Book Critics Circle Award, *The Los Angeles Times* Book Prize, the Pen Voelcker Prize, and the Pulitzer Prize. *Four-Legged Girl* was a finalist for the Pulitzer Prize. She received a 2020 Guggenheim Fellowship, and the 2021 John Updike Award from the American Academy of Arts and Letters. Seuss is a chancellor for the Academy of American Poets. Seuss's seventh collection, *Althea: Poems,* is forthcoming from Graywolf Press in 2027.

DEREK SHEFFIELD has led several birding trips over the years as part of the annual Leavenworth Spring Birdfest, and he has helped with many Audubon Christmas bird counts. The eighth poet laureate of Washington State (2025–2027), he received a 2024 Pacific Northwest Booksellers Award for *Cascadia Field Guide: Art, Ecology, Poetry.* His other collections include *Not for Luck, Through the Second Skin,* and *Dear America.* He edits poetry for *Terrain.org,* teaches English at Wenatchee Valley College, and can often be found in the woods along the eastern slopes of the Cascade Range near Leavenworth, Washington.

PEGGY SHUMAKER's recent book of elegiac poems is *Still Water Carving Light* (Red Hen Press). Her lyrical memoir is *Just Breathe Normally* (University of Nebraska Press). She's professor emerita at University of Alaska Fairbanks, and taught for many years at the Rainier Writing Workshop. She has been honored to serve as Alaska's writer laureate and as the Rasmuson Foundation's Distinguished Artist. She splits her time between Fairbanks, Alaska, and Tucson, Arizona.

CONSTANCE SIDLES is a master birder and long-time member of Birds Connect Seattle, where she has served on both the board and the Conservation Committee. Connie is on the faculty of the University of Washington (UW) as an instructor in continuing education programs. She also teaches classes for Audubon societies around the country, and has authored more than 600 published articles and is founder and president of Constancy Press. She has written four books about nature focusing on her favorite "backyard"—Montlake Fill, aka Union Bay Natural Area on the UW campus. Her latest book is *46 Views of Montlake Fill,* a collection of haiku-style poems illustrated with sumi-e paintings by renowned artist Hiroko Seki.

SCOT SIEGEL is a city planner, educator, and author of four full-length poetry collections, including *Tender Currencies* (MoonPath Press, 2025), winner of the Sally Albiso Poetry Book Award. Previous books include *The Constellation of Extinct Stars and Other Poems* (2016) and *Thousands Flee California Wildflowers* (2012), both from Salmon Poetry. Siegel works with *Writing The Land,* which pairs poets with land trusts nationwide. His poems appear in many journals and are part of the permanent public art installation along TriMet's Light Rail "Orange Line" in Portland, Oregon. He has received fellowship residencies with Playa at Summer Lake and Oregon State University's Spring Creek Project, and he previously published the poetry journal *Untitled Country Review.*

MARTHA SILANO's (1961-2025) poetry collections included *Terminal Surreal* (Acre Books, 2025) and *Last Train to Paradise: New and Selected Poems* (Saturnalia Books, 2025). Her recent publication, *This One We Call Ours,* won the 2023 Blue Lynx Prize (Lynx House Press, 2024). She also authored *Gravity Assist, Reckless Lovely,* and *The Little Office of the Immaculate Conception,* all from Saturnalia Books. Individual poems were published in *Poetry, Paris Review, American*

Poetry Review, Kenyon Review, The Missouri Review, and in many anthologies. Awards included North American Review's James Hearst Poetry Prize and The Cincinnati Review's Robert and Adele Schiff Poetry Prize. Two of her poems appeared in The Best American Poetry Series (Scribner). Martha taught at Bellevue College for 20+ years following her calling to be a teacher. She was a much loved poet among Washington State poets. More information at marthasilano.net.

RENEE SIMMS' writing has appeared in Salon, Guernica, Oxford American, The Southwest Review, The Los Angeles Times, and elsewhere. Her debut story collection, Meet Behind Mars (Wayne State University Press, 2018), was a Foreword INDIES finalist for Short Stories, featured on NPR, and the National Book Critics Circle blog, and was listed by The Root as one of twenty-eight brilliant books by Black authors in 2018. She has a memoir and a novel forthcoming from Farrar, Straus and Giroux. Renee teaches in the low residency MFA program at Pacific Lutheran University and is an Associate Professor of African American Studies at the University of Puget Sound.

JASMINÉ ELIZABETH SMITH is an Oklahoma poet, educator, and facilitator now residing in Seattle, Washington. She is a Cave Canem and 2025 National Endowment of the Arts Poetry fellow. Her poetic work interrogates the archives of the African Diaspora in various historical contexts and eras and finds the critical linkages between the past and present. Her work has twice been nominated for a Pushcart Prize and has been featured in publications such as Poetry, World Literature Today, and This is the Honey: A Contemporary Poetry Anthology of Black Poetry, among others. Her debut collection, South Flight (University of Georgia Press, 2020), was the winner of the Georgia Poetry Prize.

JOANNIE STANGELAND is the author of the poetry collections The Scene You See, In Both Hands, Into the Rumored Spring, and the prose-poem pamphlet A Piece of Work (all from Ravenna Press), and the chapbooks Weathered Steps (Rose Alley Press) and A Steady Longing for Flight (winner of the inaugural Floating Bridge Press Chapbook Award). Her poems have also appeared in *Raven Chronicles, The Pedestal Magazine, New England Review, I Sing the Salmon Home: Poems from Washington State, Purr and Yowl: An Anthology of Poetry about Cats,* and other journals and anthologies. Joannie is a two-time Pushcart nominee, and she holds an MFA from the Rainier Writing Workshop.

SARAH STOCKTON is the author of two poetry chapbooks: *Time's Apprentice* (dancing girl press) and *Castaway* (Glass Lyre Press). Her full-length collection, *The Scarecrow of My Former Self* (MoonPath Press, 2024), was a finalist for the Sally Albiso Poetry Book Award. Sarah's poems have appeared in *Poetry Northwest, Blue Mountain Review, About Place Journal, Rogue Agent,* and *Rise Up Review,* among others, and her work has appeared in several anthologies. Sarah lives on the Olympic Peninsula in the Pacific Northwest, by the Salish Sea.

MARY ELLEN TALLEY is a Seattle-based writer who has had poetry published in journals such as *Deep Wild, CIRQUE, The Fourth River,* and *Caustic Frolic,* as well as in anthologies such as *Sing the Salmon Home* and *Raising Lilly Ledbetter.* Her poems have received three Pushcart nominations. Talley's three chapbooks are: *Postcards from the Lilac City* (Finishing Line Press, 2020), *Taking Leave* (Kelsay Press, 2024), and *Infusion* (online from Red Wolf Journal, 2024). With degrees from the University of Washington, she is a former public school-based speech-language pathologist (SLP). Her website is www.maryellentalley.com.

HAROLD TAW is a playwright and multi-form writer. His debut novel was *Adventures of the Karaoke King* (Lake Union Publishing, 2011). His writing has featured on NPR, in a *New York Times* bestselling anthology, and in *The Seattle Times;* his screenplay *Dog Park* was a 2023 LA LGBTQ+ Film Festival winner. As an inaugural member of The 5th Ave Theatre's Writers Group, Harold wrote the book for *PERSUASION: A NEW MUSICAL,* which premiered at Taproot Theatre in 2017. Recent projects include a young adult trilogy (4Culture Grant), book and lyrics for a teampunk musical (4Culture Grant), and a play about digital immortality (Seattle CityArtist Grant).

ANN TEPLICK is a poet, playwright, prose writer, and teaching artist, with an MFA in writing from the Vermont College of Fine Arts. For twenty-five years she has written with youth in hospitals, psychiatric units, juvenile detention centers, public schools, and arts non-profits. Her writing has appeared in *Tahoma Literary Review, Raven Chronicles, Crab Creek Review, The Louisville Review,* and others. Her plays have been showcased in Washington, Oregon, and Nova Scotia. She's a Jack Straw and Hedgebrook alumna, and has received funding for creative projects from Artist Trust, 4Culture, Seattle Office of Arts and Culture, and The Society of Children's Book Writers and Illustrators.

BRIAN TURNER has five collections of poetry, from *Here, Bullet* to *The Dead Peasant's Handbook* (Alice James Books), and a memoir—*My Life as a Foreign Country* (W.W. Norton & Company, 2024). He's the editor of *The Kiss* and co-edited *The Strangest of Theatres.* His poems and essays have been published in *The New York Times, The Guardian, National Geographic,* and *Harper's,* among other fine journals, and he was featured in the documentary *Operation Homecoming: Writing the Wartime Experience,* nominated for an Academy Award. He lives in Florida with his dog, Dene, the world's sweetest golden retriever.

CINDY VEACH is the author of three full-length poetry collections, *Monster Galaxy* (MoonPath Press); *Her Kind* (CavanKerry Press), an Eric Hoffer Montaigne Medal finalist; *Gloved Against Blood* (CavanKerry Press), a Paterson Poetry Prize finalist and Massachusetts Center for the Book "Must Read;" and the chapbook *Innocents* (Nixes Mate). Her poems have appeared in the Academy of American Poets *Poem-a-Day, AGNI, Michigan Quarterly Review, North American Review, Poet Lore, Nimrod International Journal,* and elsewhere. She is the recipient of the Philip Booth Prize and Samuel Allen Washington Prize. Cindy is co-poetry editor of *MER.*

DAVID WAGONER (1926–2021) was born in Massillon, Ohio. He is the author of numerous poetry collections, including *Good Morning and Good Night* (University of Illinois Press, 2005);

The House of Song (University of Illinois Press, 2002); *Traveling Light: Collected and New Poems* (University of Illinois Press, 1999); and *Through the Forest: New and Selected Poems* (Atlantic Monthly Press, 1987). Wagoner's *Collected Poems, 1956–1976* (Indiana University Press, 1976) was nominated for the National Book Award in 1977. Wagoner received an American Academy of Arts and Letters Award, the Sherwood Anderson Award, the Fels Prize, the Ruth Lilly Poetry Prize, the Eunice Tjetjens Memorial Award, and English-Speaking Union prizes, as well as fellowships from the Ford Foundation, the Guggenheim Foundation, and the National Endowment for the Arts. A former Chancellor of the Academy of American Poets, Wagoner was the editor of *Poetry Northwest* from 1966 to 2002.

CHERYL WAITKEVICH spent forty years working in healthcare. Now retired, she is enrolled in the Rainier Writers Workshop, the MFA program at Pacific Lutheran University. She has been published in *West Trestle Review, Galway Review, River Heron Review, Innisfree Poetry Journal,* as well as other journals. She lives in Olympia, Washington, with her husband Robert Jorgensen.

KATHARINE WHITCOMB is the author of three full-length collections of poetry, including *Habitats*, published in January 2024 from Poetry NW Editions in the Possession Sound Series; *Saints of South Dakota & Other Poems,* which won the Bluestem Award, chosen by Lucia Perillo; and *The Daughter's Almanac,* which won the Backwaters Prize, chosen by Patricia Smith. She has published two poetry chapbooks and a book of faux self-help/art criticism, titled *The Art Courage Program.* She was a Stegner Fellow at Stanford University and is the recipient of fellowships from the Fine Arts Work Center in Provincetown and elsewhere. She is a Distinguished Professor at Central Washington University. After living twenty years in Washington State, she now makes her home in northern Vermont.

JANE WONG is the author of the memoir *Meet Me Tonight in Atlantic City* (Tin House, 2023), winner of the Washington State Book Award. She also wrote two poetry collections: *How to Not Be Afraid of Everything* (Alice James, 2021) and *Overpour*

(Action Books, 2016). She is the recipient of a Pushcart Prize and fellowships and residencies from the U.S. Fulbright Program, Harvard's Woodberry Poetry Room, Artist Trust, Hedgebrook, Ucross, Loghaven, the Barbara Deming Memorial Fund, and others. An interdisciplinary artist as well, she has exhibited her poetry installations and performances at the Frye Art Museum, Richmond Art Gallery, and the Asian Art Museum. She grew up in a take-out restaurant on the Jersey shore and is an Associate Professor at Western Washington University.

SANDRA YANNONE, Poet Laureate of Old Saybrook, Connecticut, and retired Faculty Writing Center Director at The Evergreen State College, is the author of *The Glass Studio* (2024) and *Boats for Women* (2019), both from Salmon Poetry in Ireland. Her writings appear in print and online internationally in *Ploughshares, Poetry Ireland Review, Seattle Review, Calyx,* and the *Washington State Queer Poetry Anthology,* among others. She is co-editor of the forthcoming *Unsinkable: Poems Inspired by the Titanic* (Salmon Poetry Press, 2026), and the series editor for Seven Kitchen Press's A.V. Christie Chapbook Series. In March, 2020, she co-founded the online reading series Cultivating Voices LIVE Poetry. She also co-hosts *Last Tuesdays with Sandy and Thomas* for the Olympia Poetry Network. Visit her at www.sandrayannone.com.

NATHAN YOCKEY is a poetry and short fiction writer from Prince of Wales Island, Alaska. He enjoys writing about his home and the subsistence lifestyle of Southeast Alaska. Nathan has been published in *Arcturus Literary Magazine* and *Elysian Literary Magazine,* and he won Highline College's 2020 Student Poetry Contest.

MAYA JEWELL ZELLER is the author, most recently, of the forthcoming *Raised by Ferns* (Porphyry Press, Spring 2026); *The Wonder of Mushrooms* (AdventureKEEN, September 2025); the textbook *Advanced Poetry: A Writer's Guide and Anthology* (Bloomsbury, 2024); and the poetry collection, *out takes/ glove box* (New American Press, 2023), which was selected by Eduardo Corral as winner of the New American Poetry Prize. Maya's work has received fellowships from the

University of Oxford, Washington State Artist Trust, Centrum, and the Sustainable Arts Foundation. Maya teaches for Central Washington University and Western Colorado University. Learn more at mayajewellzeller.com.

BIOGRAPHICAL NOTES: EDITORIAL STAFF

DR. STEPHANIE DELANEY (Bird Notes) loves all things birds. She is studying birding through Birds Connect Seattle and has been birding seriously since the pandemic, submitting birds most days in eBird, with over 1500 reports submitted to date. Stephanie is a lifelong learner and higher education administrator. She is especially interested in urban birding and teaching more diverse audiences the joys of the bird world.

SUSAN RICH (Editor) is the author of six collections of poetry and co-editor of two prose anthologies. Her most recent poetry books include *Blue Atlas* (Red Hen Press) and *Gallery of Postcards and Maps: New and Selected Poems* (Salmon Poetry). In addition, she has co-edited the anthologies *Demystifying the Manuscript: Creating a Book of Poems* (Two Sylvias Press) and *Strangest of Theatres: Poets Crossing Borders* (McSweeney's). Educated at Harvard University, University of Oregon, and the University of Massachusetts, Susan's previous books include *Cloud Pharmacy, The Alchemist's Kitchen, Cures Include Travel,* and *The Cartographer's Tongue—Poems of the World.* A recipient of the PEN USA Award and the Times Literary Supplement Award (London), she has also received recognition from the Fulbright Foundation and Peace Corps Writers. Rich's recent poetry appears in the *New England Review, Ploughshares, Poetry Northwest,* and elsewhere. She lives and writes in West Seattle, Washington.

HIROKO SEKI (Artist) is a Nihonga and Sumi-e artist. Seki: "My sumi-ink history started with sumi-ink hand-drawn, silk-textile, Yuzen kimono painting, an academic degree, and, most importantly, studying under sumi-e master, Ota Shoukoh. I got my artist name Shuhkoh from her. I enshrine moments from nature. Nature draws in my senses. Sumi-ink, soy, and dye drive innovation in my Sumi-e." hiroko@shuhkoh.com

URSULA VALDEZ (Foreword) is an avian ecologist and conservationist. Born and raised in Peru, she grew up fascinated by nature. In particular, she developed an appreciation of birds, wildlife, and the forest from her father and her naturalist grandmother. Ursula studied biology in Lima, Peru, going on to earn graduate degrees at North Carolina State University and the University of Washington. Dr. Valdez has worked in six countries researching and teaching about birds and their habitats. Currently, she works at the UW Bothell, teaching ecology in a myriad of modalities as well as short courses for Birds Connect Seattle. She returns to Peru each summer to teach Peruvian students varied research and conservation methods. When she is not working, you can find Ursula birding, hiking, making pottery, and gardening where she grows food for humans, birds, and pollinators. Ursula lives in Seattle with her husband, Todd.

OTHER RAVEN BOOKS AND PUBLICATIONS

Positively Uncivilized, essays by Rena Priest
  Paperback, ISBN 979-8-9914032-3-8
  eBook, ISBN 979-8-9914032-4-5

FUTURE X, science fiction by Georg Koszulinski
  Paperback, ISBN 979-8-9914032-1-4
  eBook, ISBN 979-8-9914032-2-1

Treasures in Heaven, Raven 2nd edition, fiction by
Kathleen Alcalá
  Paperback, ISBN 978-1-735480-6-7
  eBook, ISBN 979-8-9914032-0-7

*This Light Called Darkness, A Raven Chronicles Anthology,
Selected Work* 1997–2005, Eds. Kathleen Alcalá, Phoebe Bosché,
Paul Hunter, and Anna Odessa Linzer
  Paperback, ISBN 978-1-7354780-4-3

*Poem of Stone and Bone: The Iconography of James W.
Washington Jr. in Fourteen Stanzas and Thirty-One Days*,
by Carletta Carrington Wilson
  Paperback, ISBN 978-1-7354780-2-9

The Flower in the Skull, Raven 2nd edition, fiction by
Kathleen Alcalá
  Paperback, ISBN 978-1-7354780-3-6
  eBook, ISBN 978-1-7354780-5-0

Words from the Café: An Anthology, Raven 2nd edition, edited
by Anna Bálint, photographs by Willie J. Pugh
  Paperback, ISBN 978-0-9979468-9-5

Spirits of the Ordinary, A Tale of Casas Grandes, Raven 2nd
edition, fiction by Kathleen Alcalá
  Paperback, ISBN 987-0-9979468-8-8
  eBook, ISBN 987-0-9979468-6-4

Take a Stand: Art Against Hate, A Raven Chronicles Anthology (Winner of the 2021 Washington State Book Award for Poetry), edited by Anna Bálint, Phoebe Bosché, and Thomas Hubbard
  Paperback, ISBN 978-0-9979468-7-1

Stealing Light, A Raven Chronicles Anthology, Selected Work 1991–1996, Edited by Kathleen Alcalá, Phoebe Bosché, Paul Hunter, and Stephanie Lawyer
  Paperback, ISBN 978-0-9979468-5-7

PUBLISHER'S ACKNOWLEDGMENTS

Raven is indebted to our 2025 Co-Sponsors for partial funding of our programs: the City of Seattle Office of Arts & Culture (Centering Arts & Racial Equity (C.A.R.E.); 4Culture (Sustained Support, through King County Lodging Tax and Doors Open funding). Thanks to all those who donated during the GIVE BIG 2025 Campaign for their generous donations in support of Raven publications and programs:

Crows: Kathleen Alcalá, Frances McCue

Steller's Jays: Susan Deer Cloud

Mockingbirds: Anonymous, Risa Denenberg, Sharon Hashimoto, Paul C. Hunter, Sibyl James, Larry Laurence, Joannie Stangeland, Harold Taw

Rooks: Lenora Good, Anna Linzer, John Mifsud, Mary Ellen Talley

Jackdaws: Rachel Beatty, Natalie Pascale Boisseau, Bethany Reid, Susan Pace, Kathleen Flenniken, Diane Glancy, Sheryl Sirotnik

Magpies: Rachel Harrington

—Phoebe Bosché
Managing Editor, Raven Chronicles Press

4
CULTURE

4
CULTURE

KING COUNTY DOORS OPEN

A&
OFFICE OF ARTS & CULTURE
SEATTLE

www.ingramcontent.com/pod-product-compliance
Lightning Source LLC
Chambersburg PA
CBHW041932260326
41914CB00010B/1271